THE DUNDEE HANDBOOK

Author Information

Fiona Danskin was born and brought up in Dundee. She studied at Duncan of Jordanstone College of Art and painted for many years before pursuing a career as an actor. Fiona started writing her first book, *Jungle Adventure*, at the age of nine, but writer's block prevented her from progressing beyond page five. Thanks to the constant incentive of fine pints and good food throughout this project, history has not repeated itself.

THE

DUNDEE
HANDBOOK

what to do and where to do it

Fiona Danskin

MAINSTREAM
PUBLISHING

EDINBURGH AND LONDON

First published in Great Britain in 2002 by
MAINSTREAM PUBLISHING COMPANY (EDINBURGH) LTD
7 Albany Street
Edinburgh EH1 3UG

ISBN 1 84018 459 0

A catalogue record for this book is available from the British Library

Typeset in Futurist and Stone Print
Printed and bound in Great Britain by
Cox & Wyman Ltd

My Fellow Pub Dog

The birth of the idea and much of the initial pub research for this book was a joint effort between myself and my fellow pub dog, Kath Clark. I'd like to thank her, and acknowledge her involvement, support and written contributions.

———————————

ACKNOWLEDGEMENTS

Thanks to Chris Biddlecombe for contributions, and immense and unwavering support.

Also to Malcolm J. Thomson, Jason Nelson, Mike Kane, Colin Danskin, Peggy Marra, Pat, John and Ewan, all drinking and eating companions (you know who you are), and all pub dogs and their human guardians.

Contents

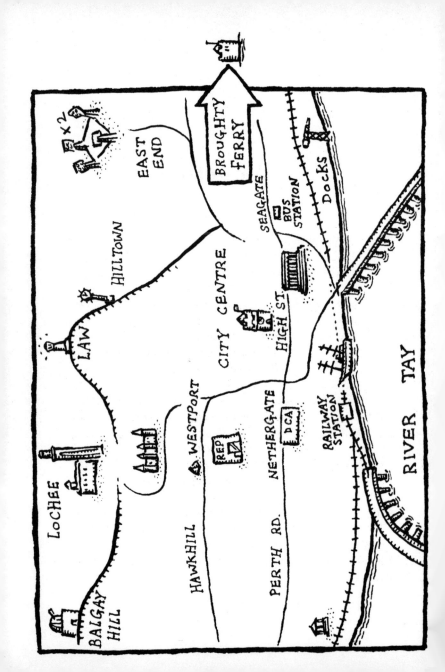

Introduction

First of all, I'd just like to make it clear that no pub, restaurant, or any other establishment mentioned in this guide had prior knowledge to of its publication, and as such, no one has paid to be included, or advertised or sponsored it in any way. While going about my pub and restaurant research, there was always at least one other drinker with me: either Kath or any number of other drinking and eating chums – hence occasional references to 'we' rather than just 'I'. I hope this doesn't confuse, but I'd hate you to think of me supping alone. Also, as I have no vested interest in any places reviewed, it is therefore a completely independent and honest appraisal. Right, that's the formalities out of the way.

This is not a book about Dundee's past. This has been done many times before by those who know about such things. There are no historical discourses, other than the odd bit of nostalgia, and no musings about the future. This book is about Dundee's present – how it is now and, more importantly, how to enjoy it. Most of it is based on personal opinion and experience – and undoubtedly there will be things which you disagree with, but I think it's clear that I've assessed everything fairly, and have listened to other folk's thoughts and wise words on particular topics. Whether you agree or disagree, I hope you have as much fun trying out new places as I did researching them. Happy exploring.

DUNDEE: A BRIEF INTRODUCTION

Dundee. Also known as the 'City of Discovery' (one big ship on an icy expedition and you have a whole new catchphrase), 'Land o' Cakes', (home of the famous 'peh'), 'Naples of the North', and 'The Three Js' – the rather lame and misleading slogan the city was labelled with for years, due to its success with jute, jam (well, marmalade really) and journalism. Only one of these remains now – journalism, in the form of D.C. Thomson, producers of fine publications such as *The Beano*, *The Dandy*, *The Evening Telegraph* (known as 'the *Tully*'), and of course *The Sunday Post*. These have between them spawned some of Dundee's most famous characters: Dennis the Menace, Desperate Dan, The Bash Street Kids, Oor Wullie and The Broons. Unfortunately these are no longer allowed simply to remain great creations in your Saturday comic, but have turned up all over the city in the form of sculptures, advertising for the Discovery Centre, wraparounds for litter bins, and special Christmas light displays. As you approach Dundee, you will be greeted with the city's name in cartoon lettering. With an award-winning new Arts Centre, Dundee Contemporary Arts (DCA), being one of the main attractions for visitors (as well as being one of the best in the UK), it's really time we grew up. Introducing the award ceremony for the 2000 Turner Prize, Nicholas Serrota named DCA as one of the leading art centres/galleries in the UK, and it was the only Scottish gallery mentioned. Not bad for a city with a reputation for cultural stagnation.

Dundee has a fantastic and unique outlook. Being built along the length of the River Tay, it has spectacular views south to Fife and the Lomond Hills, north to the Sidlaws, and west to the Carse of Gowrie. On a clear day you can see forever (well, almost . . . from the top of The Law, you can just about see a hole-in-one on the 18th green in St Andrews).

As you approach Dundee from Fife you come across one of two unusually long bridges, both giving you a good overall shape of the city. General Ulysses Grant once paid a visit to Dundee, an occasion celebrated in a song by Dundee singer-songwriter Michael Marra, in which General Grant remarks, 'What a mighty long bridge to such a mighty little ole town.' Not such a little ole town any more, but still a mighty long bridge.

Unfortunately, your visual introduction is the monstrous Tayside House, the Stalinist Olympia Leisure Centre, the Hilton (a grey cube disguised as a hotel) and the back end of the Mecca bingo – more *Close Encounters* than two fat ladies, although its towers, seen from the front, are listed. Don't be put off by this rather gloomy entrance; there are some wee treasures behind the façade.

More Thoughts on the City

Dundee gets a bad press; people don't even have to have visited the city before they're ready to denounce it. I often work in Edinburgh and Glasgow, and inevitably it comes to light that I'm not 'one of them'. The fact that not only do I have Dundee blood, but also that I choose to continue to live there is inevitably met with 'Why Dundee? Armpit of Scotland, isn't it?', or an equally derogatory remark. At this point, I will ask them, as politely as can be expected, if they've ever been to Dundee. The answer is usually, 'Well, no, but . . .' I rest my case. It's like saying you don't like tattie scones when you haven't even tried them. I know we're not the only city to suffer from this presumptive dismissal, but Dundee truly is on the way up. There's the regeneration of the city centre, the pioneering cancer research centres, some stunning new architecture and the success of Dundee Contemporary Arts for starters. It's also home to one of the UK's top art colleges, two universities, and Scotland's first purpose-built, full-time dance school. And let's not forget that we have two Scottish Premier League football teams (actually, at the time of writing, 'on-the-up' probably doesn't apply here, but more of that later . . .).

Broughty Ferry

Broughty Ferry is about four miles east of Dundee. It's a seaside town which has reluctantly accepted its place as a Dundee suburb. On the whole 'the Ferry' is quite posh, compared to many parts of Dundee, but not in the way St Andrews is posh (i.e. a university town majoring in non-Scots). Most people in the Ferry are Scottish, if not Dundonian. It is an eclectic mix of big villas, many built by the city's jute barons, and small fishermen's cottages along the shoreline. Far less spoilt than Dundee, there's a stony beach, a sandy beach, a fifteenth-century castle, some swans, a lifeboat, seaweed, sea smells, seashells, wee waterfront cottages, the best ice cream, and some of the best pubs in Dundee. As it stretches north-east it becomes Barnhill and Monifieth.

Broughty Ferry used to have its own cinema, The Regal, which eventually went part-time, operating half the week as a cinema and the other half as a bingo hall. Bingo won in the end, and it's now a garage. You can easily walk or cycle to the Ferry from Dundee. The most pleasant route hugs the riverside and takes you past the Royal Tay Yacht Club. In fact, I would recommend the walk in order to appreciate the Ferry's abundance of marvellous public houses, and pints therein.

Housing Schemes

As is the case in every city, Dundee has many housing schemes. In Fintry, you will probably get lost, as every street begins with 'Fin–', as with Douglas, where a remarkable 80 streets begin with 'Bal–'. Charleston, Menzieshill, Whitfield, Ardler, St Marys and Happyhillock (never has somewhere been so inappropriately named) are areas that if you live in Dundee, you will know already; if you're visiting, you most likely won't be going to them anyway.

Lochee, on the other hand, is definitely worth a visit. Existing largely within Lochee High Street, this is a wee town in itself, with its own swimming-pool, bike shop, good second-hand shops and a Fisher & Donaldson bakers. It has some old pubs, and is the gateway to Camperdown and beyond. Camperdown Works was once Dundee's largest jute works and existed as a small self-sufficient town with housing for the workers, and its own shops. The glorious Cox's Stack still dominates the skyline here. The works lay empty for many years before being turned into a sort of leisure park, with a bowling alley, a nightclub (which lasted about 15 minutes), and an Odeon multiplex cinema. The cinema has since closed, with the building of a supposedly bigger and better venue even further out of town. More of cinemas later. One of Dundee's many Tesco stores is also at Camperdown Works.

Dundee is increasingly being recognised as a thriving community, and as a city worth visiting in its own right. Travel guides used to dismiss Dundee, siting it merely as a convenient place to base yourself whilst taking in the other, bonnier sights. These days, it's demanding a bit more attention for itself, and at last is being given the praise it deserves, as the following quotes will testify.

From *The Rough Guide to Scotland*,
fifth edition, 2002.

'Dundee itself, although not the most obvious tourist destination, has in recent years become a more dynamic and progressive city, and makes for a less snooty alternative to Aberdeen . . . a refreshingly unpretentious and welcoming city, wonderfully placed on the banks of the Tay.'

From *Footprint Guide to Scotland*,
second edition, 2002

'Few cities in Britain can match Dundee's impressive setting, seen at its breathtaking best from across the Tay, in Fife. But, despite the common consensus that the views of the city are indeed spectacular, certain

> guide-books have suggested that visitors keep their
> distance. Which just goes to show how out of touch
> they are, for Dundee has transformed itself into a
> vibrant, thriving city and an increasingly popular
> destination for tourists.'

And one of my favourites:

> 'But the city's best-kept secret is its people. The
> accent may at first be somewhat impenetrable but
> Dundonians have an endearing earthy humour and
> are the friendliest bunch of people you'll find
> anywhere on the east coast of Scotland.'

One of the best things about Dundee is that it's so walkable. Unless you're really tired, in a desperate hurry, or for any other reason can't do the walking thing, virtually anywhere can be reached on foot. Apart from its hilliness, it's great seen on a bike too. Whether you live in the west end of the city, or the east, you have no excuse not to dip your toe into the other side. The city centre itself is incredibly compact, which is great when you realise you've forgotten to pick up your free-range eggs from Tayhealth (see p159) on a Saturday afternoon. Dundee has a pretty good bus service, should you be going out to one of its many housing schemes, Broughty Ferry, or further afield into Angus, Perthshire, or Fife.

1

Where to Drink

INTRODUCTION

Are you looking for your first pint in Dundee, or perhaps your last? Are you a local stuck in a pub rut? If so, this is the chapter for you. What follows is our own account of, and thoughts on, a number of Dundee and Broughty Ferry pubs.

It's fair to say that we like pubs. Indeed, it was drinking in a certain pub for the first time that prompted us to put pen to paper. There are many pubs you may not yet have – indeed may never – visit (and in some cases for good reason), but, believe us, there are fresh pastures out there for you Dundee drinkers. Although our initial idea was to write a guide to all the pubs of Dundee, we soon realised that Dundee needed a guide-book which explored much more than just its drinking dens. Naturally, we had to limit the number of pubs to include in the guide. Given that we are quite particular in our tastes, it only seems fair to state our preferences. No doubt this will give rise to much debate, as your own criteria and experiences may be very different from ours. Obviously, all our old favourites are here, along with some new ones, but also included are what we hope is a broad selection of Dundee's other watering-holes. Cheers!

General Likes and Dislikes about Pubs

Music: Good if either absent altogether, or unobtrusive and at a low enough level not to cause hoarseness when communicating.

Karaoke: Not high on our list of entertainment. However, knowing that many people enjoy singing Shirley Bassey in public (and that's just the blokes), we have mentioned, where necessary, pubs which encourage this activity.

Beer: A decent selection of beer and lager is essential; independent brewery ales are far superior, and pubs offering changing guest ales, or cask conditioned ones are in the winning lane. Many pubs we like don't offer this, but the large brewery ales they do have are kept well and are more than palatable. Inclusion of a good premium lager as well as a 'cooking' one is also a bonus.

Wine: On draught this is not good, although it is often found in many top-notch pubs. Just don't drink the stuff.

Staff: The best pubs have staff who evidently enjoy their work, and have a knowledge of what they're pouring for you. Good banter with customers is always a good sign, as is a good social mix of customers.

Pub architecture: Open fires are good, so are very high or very low ceilings, wooden floors, old linoleum, nicotine-stained cornicing and original brewery mirrors. Old pubs are generally the best pubs for pub architecture. As with beer, there are a few exceptions and some very plain pubs we visited had a great atmosphere, which is something you can't design. We are not keen on chrome, or fridges full of fluorescent bottled drinks.

Dogs: A sign of a good pub is a pub dog in the corner – often a mongrel, drinking Guinness out of an ashtray. Toots, one of our featured 'pub dogs', drinks in the Campbeltown Bar, which is very popular with Dundee pub dogs and drinkers alike.

Supermarket Pubs: Not a good thing, and not to be confused with brewery-owned pubs, many of which are great. The supermarket pub is one which is part of a large chain, such as Wetherspoons, or Yates. Like their grocery namesakes, these places are stripped of character and individuality, and because of their conglomerate nature can afford to charge far less than their independent cousins. A pub should be somewhere that does more than just sell booze, however cheaply. The social aspect is paramount, and the best atmospheres will be found far away from these soulless barns.

DUNDEE PUBS BY AREA

Pubs are listed by area as follows:
  City Centre
  Perth Road and Nethergate
  Hawkhill and Westport
  East End and Hilltown
  Lochee
  Broughty Ferry
Pubs are listed alphabetically within their area.

City Centre

ANGUS LOUNGE
39 Union Street
Tel: 01382 203559

After struggling through the very narrow, but rather sweet, wooden swing doors, I found myself in what must surely be the smallest pub in Dundee. Owned by ex-Dundee United footballer Davy Dodds, there is, refreshingly, no football memorabilia around the walls, but instead a black-and-white photo of Charlie Chaplin. The size of a small living-room, this is a friendly wee place, with its lino floor and small zig-zag of seats, which reflects the narrowness of the doorway. There were two groups of folk there along with us – one young and mainly female, the other middle-aged men, so a good mixed clientele. Staff were friendly and, although the selection of brews was unremarkable, they served up a decent pint of McEwan's 80/-. The ladies' toilet was one of the most individual I've come across on my pub travels – as ever, space saving. It wasn't unlike a ship's cabin, with its varnished wood-panelled walls, and a wee sliding door.

In the daytime, the Angus Lounge is a popular hide-out with old boys. Downstairs is the Rendezvous, where I'm told much singing and partying goes on, particularly at weekends.

ARCTIC BAR
3–5 New Entry Inn
Tel: 01382 226740

We were very excited about visiting the Arctic, having read the following on the Dundee Licensed Trade Association website: 'A main feature of the pub is a centrepiece in the floor of the old bar depicting a polar bear on top of an iceberg.' How could we have been unaware of such an intriguing pub sculpture? After tying up the huskies outside, and admiring the blue plastic icebergs which adorn the exterior of the Arctic, we immediately enquired as to the whereabouts of this fantastic polar bear, and were directed to the smaller of the two bars. It took us a while to spot it – it was in fact a flat lino-esque relief set into the floor, and not the Michelangelo bear we had built up in our heads. Despite this initial disappointment, we enjoyed our visit. The sole barman on duty was friendly and very informative about the pub's history. There's a sparseness about the Arctic, including the staff, clientele, drinks selection and décor. What you see is what you get here, which is what we liked about it. This pub doesn't pretend to be anything other than what it is. It's a local's local, and is pretty basic, but has a curious charm about it. We were particularly impressed with the large selection of (display only) Dundee United wines behind the bar. There is also an entertaining bunch of photos of locals around the walls.

BANK BAR
7–9 Union Street
Tel: 01382 205037

Phew. Literally three days before finishing the book, the Hogshead turned into the Bank Bar, so there was just time to write a few words. The Hogshead was a faux traditional pub with the blessing of not having a 'theme'. The Bank Bar has kept much of the appearance of its predecessor – wooden floors, thick beams, brickwork pillars and the 'old' glass panels between the seating booths. Unfortunately, the fact that this used to be a bank has been laid on with a trowel. It's unnecessarily themed, with black-and-white photos of Dundee banks, which are really not very interesting. There is also a load of framed banknotes and coins, and some photocopied articles from local newspapers about attempted bank raids.

They make up for this overdose by serving some fine beer – Boddingtons, Flowers, Old Speckled Hen and Caledonian 80/- are all on draught. Music-wise, expect anything from Tom Jones to PIL – fine choices, if a little incongruous in the setting. Open from 9 a.m. for breakfast, you can enjoy scrambled eggs and bacon butties before you embark on your first pint.

BREAD
33–37 Constitution Road
Tel: 01382 322010

This used to be called the Breadalbane Arms, although when I first frequented it many years ago, it was known as the Bothy. We always drank in the upstairs part, which doesn't exist any more, due to a fire some time ago, but I have some fond memories of those early Bothy days. A woman called Mary used to stand at the bottom of the stairs to vet the customers, and there was often live music – I vaguely remember a band called the High Cheekers, although this could easily have been somewhere else. Whatever, it was a great wee pub back then. Many changes have taken place in the interim period, and the Bread is currently one of the 'It's a Scream' pubs which are cluttering up our streets. It is best described as a slightly upmarket student union bar; I think we were probably the only people in there who weren't at Abertay University. We knew it, and so did everybody else – facial hair and sensible winter clothing being a bit of a give-away. It's very activity based, with four televisions and one big screen (all then showing boxing), tons of gaming machines and two red pool tables. It offers lots of drinks promotions, and karaoke and quiz nights. We unintentionally visited on 'It's a pound' night, where – you've guessed it – everything's a pound. We hadn't planned to stay here long, so ordered a couple of halves; the barmaid looked at us as if we were completely insane, and insisted we had pints, as they were 'only a pound'. Fair enough, but the beer wasn't all that great. Most folk seemed to be drinking bottles of 'stuff', some of which looked like mouthwash. Appropriately, the boys were drinking 'Blue' and the girls drinking 'Red'; how wonderfully old-fashioned. For a student bar, it's probably fine, and seems popular, although this may be influenced by the 'It's a pound' theme. Strange decision to install a picture window which looks on to the university car park.

BUSH BAR
30 Seagate
Tel: 01382 877891

Having not frequented this pub for many years, it was a pleasant surprise to find it in fine traditional fettle, with so many older pubs having been tidied up beyond recognition. The Bush used to be a regular haunt for people from the Seagate Gallery/Printmakers Workshop, and many a Friday night found the Bush filled to capacity with the overspill from exhibition openings. Alas, the gallery is no longer there, and the Bush has undergone a facelift in recent years. It may not have the earthy eclecticism of days gone by, but the upgrades are tasteful, if a bit clean and regular, and it's one of the more pleasant pubs in the city centre for a quieter pint or two. Some curious contemporary paintings of other Dundee pubs grace the walls.

The landlord was very friendly and hospitable and was happy to enter into a lager banter with us. The ale selection was a bit lacking, but they served up a quaffable pint of 70/- and a drinkable cooking lager (both Tennent's). Also, some good whiskies to tempt us on future visits.

The night of our first visit, there was a Manchester United European Cup game on TV, which determined the clientele (five old blokes). We were a bit alarmed to find such a small pub with three TVs – strategically placed to ensure no one would miss a kick of the Sturm Graz, we presume. There are newspapers for customers in the unlikely event they can't see the telly.

CHAMBERS
59–61 Gellatly Street
Tel: 01382 225616

The original Chambers was on the corner of Castle Street and Exchange Street, and, although never a regular, I did have a soft spot for it. Friday and Saturday nights were always good, particularly if Dundee's best-ever covers band, Mafia, was playing. I remember with fondness their version of 'Extra! Extra! Read All About It', and their fab brass section. It closed down many years ago, and there is now a new Chambers. Live music is still the thing, with (mostly covers) bands playing four nights a week, from Thursday to Sunday. There's a proper wee stage here, so they take it pretty seriously. It's very popular, especially at weekends, with the older 'rocker' – it's hard to tell these days, but I'd guess 35 to 50 is the average age here. The place is full of happy folk having a good time, with much spontaneous dancing going on. Should you tire, there are some nice seating booths where you can rest until you're ready to take to the floor again. The décor is suitably musically themed, with the walls covered in framed photos and album covers (you know, those 12-inch vinyl ones) – Kate Bush, Black Sabbath and Roy Orbison all putting in an appearance – and a couple of saxophones and a drum are stapled to the front of the bar. There is the usual selection of beers and spirits. This is a busy, lively pub, but not for those in search of a quiet Saturday-night pint.

CLUB BAR
47 Union Street
Tel: 01382 223011

Having walked past the Club Bar on literally hundreds of occasions en route to the train station, it was with a certain amount of trepidation that we stepped over their threshold. With mirrored windows and frosted glass in the door, we wondered if they had something to hide. We pushed open the door (you first, no *you* first . . .) only to be met by very friendly bar staff, and not the wild-west-conversation-stopping-strangers-in-our-midst response we were presumptuous enough to have expected. It's pretty much a locals' bar, but we were made to feel welcome and had a decent pint into the bargain.

COUNTING HOUSE
67–71 Reform Street
Tel: 01382 203822

The Counting House is a member of the Wetherspoons chain, and you pretty much know what you're going to get here. A very, very large pub, with serial drinking, a lack of atmosphere, and the lighting is so severe, you could probably rear turkeys, which would at least give the place a focus. Another of Dundee's former banks, I'd personally rather extend my overdraft and go somewhere with a bit of character. These are the supermarkets of the pub world. They can afford to sell their beer cheaply, at the expense of the smaller independent pub. Fair enough, you can get an OK pint here for a good price, but we'd rather head down the road and spend an extra tuppence on an independent pint. Also, it's a three-mile round trip to the loos, and with all that cheap booze on offer, you can bet your Bacardi Breezer you'll be clocking up the miles.

Wetherspoons have recently obtained another site in the City Centre – right next door to Yates. I am unavailable for comment.

HUXTERS
34 Reform Street
Tel: 01382 226552

Everyone likes to go on holiday. Few of us, however, choose the hotel reception or airport lounge as our final destination – which Huxters strongly resembles. Formerly The Old Bank Bar, this was converted from bank into pub by the Morrison family, who more recently made another, far superior, bank conversion with the establishment of the Trades House Bar (see p.32). Sadly the grand-old-house feel of the Old Bank has been lost, and replaced with something far less gentle on the eyes. With the carpet and furnishings fighting for your attention, it's an assault on the senses. There is an attempt at classiness with an alarming selection of art prints, such as a Rothko in a gold frame. There are still some great features, such as the cornices and some of the plasterwork, although this has now been painted peach, and is reminiscent of a *Changing Rooms* makeover. At night, the music is as loud as the décor.

Cheap pub grub is available, with cheese and peas featuring highly, and you can get a sausage sandwich for £1.95. Cocktails are a speciality and, with 'Erection' and 'Blow Job' on offer, it should come as no surprise that Huxters is busy at the weekend. Curious mix of hanging baskets and bouncers outside.

JAFFRAY'S
22 St Andrews Street
Tel: 01382 223923

An improvement on its predecessor, Grissel Jaffray's, with the witchcraft theme thankfully toned down. (According to local folklore, Grissel Jaffray was a local witch who was burnt at the stake, just round the corner). The prints of fifteenth-century unpleasantries have been replaced with an odd collection of framed prints, with bunches of grapes and Stonehenge hanging side by side. A stack of very large fake books are tucked into a corner – presumably these are intended to emulate dusty old spell books. Jaffray's still seems to suffer from a lack of customers, although Saturday nights are busier. Still, it's the only pub I've seen advertising a 'winter sale'. A karaoke man was desperately trying to get folk up to sing, with little success. Yellow on the outside, bright on the inside, this is a harmless pub with very cheery bar staff. It's got the usual beers, three malts, and is very handy for the bus station.

MACDANIELS
34–36 Whitehall Crescent
Tel: 01382 221803

This pub started out life as Jack Daniels, but a cunning play on words has transformed it into the somewhat cheesy MacDaniels. We visited twice midweek, and it was reminiscent of the *Marie Celeste*, despite numerous drinks promotions and happy hours. It seemed a mystery that it remained open, but we heard mutterings about it being busier on a weekend, so being the fair-minded folk that we are, we gave it the benefit of the doubt, and rewarded it with a third visit one Saturday night. It was indeed a more spirited atmosphere, mainly due to the evidently popular covers/wedding band belting out 'Mustang Sally' and David Gray songs, despite the fact they were playing in a den of chairs and tables, and in virtual darkness. There was even a couple of folk having a wee dance. Without the lure of live bands, I'm not sure how MacD's would survive, but everyone likes a good tune and all that. The décor is an odd mishmash of styles, with particularly horrible '80s function-suite chairs, and a curious cosy corner like a living-room installation, complete with mantelpiece and wally dugs. Pleasant enough staff, and an unremarkable beer selection. Specialities are lethal-sounding shooters and cocktails.

MERCANTILE
100–108 Commercial Street
Tel: 01382 225500

Another former Morrison family pub, the Mercantile used to have a great reputation and was well known for its excellent range of ales. Visiting for the first time in a few years, I found the situation much changed. This, presumably, is due to the Mercantile having been left in the hands of a chain. Rumour has it that it may be changing hands again, so who knows what the future holds. The only beer they had on offer, other than the usual selection of 80/-, Guinness, etc., was Boddingtons Bitter, and it was off. I was quite underwhelmed by the pub, finding it neither likeable nor dislikeable. It's a bit of a guddle really and, although it's a big pub, its layout doesn't allow you to get a real sense of the space. It physically goes off in so many different directions, with a slightly raised area to the left of the bar, an upstairs balcony space for waitress-service dining, and numerous wee pockets and corners which all seem disconnected from one another. I imagine it's a fine pub to visit in a large group, and seems popular with the after-work suit crowd. Our barman didn't seem particularly interested in us or his job – not that we're necessarily that interesting, but a smile wouldn't go amiss. What we did like was its vast collection of old photographs of Dundee, including a lovely aerial view of the Howff in winter, and one of the old Empress Ballroom (long gone). Also some old advertisements, including one for Valentines, a local firm who used to produce greetings cards, and actually employed folk to write the awful verses inside. The music is fairly loud and anonymous. They do have a very good range of malt whiskies, although I suspect a step ladder is required to fetch them down. Not for those in a hurry.

O'NEILLS
80 North Lindsay Street
Tel: 01382 205931

The first of the invasion of Irish theme pubs and, appropriately, the only survivor. I was pleasantly surprised to find that what I'd remembered as a typical Irish theme pub – one of those with beds hanging from the ceiling, and old boots and saucepans everywhere – has been stripped of all that nonsense. It's a big, sparse-looking pub, but it's not without warmth, and has the feeling of an old meeting hall. With its wooden floorboards, tables and chairs, and an extremely long wooden bar, you almost expect to find shamrocks on the floor and sawdust on the Guinness (or should that be the other way around? Hard to tell after a few of those). It's got an eclectic mix of lighting fixtures, including some nice old glass lampshades. A pretty lively place, with a predominantly student clientele. Live bands are a regular occurrence, usually Irish or folky in nature, with the odd jigger jollying things along. The night we were in, a snail race was due to start at 10 p.m. It looked like it was all off, but with a minute to spare, a small gang of them turned up, with bubble wrap over their shells. Slows them down, apparently.

No surprises with the beer: Guinness, Murphy's and Caffrey's, and a selection of Irish whiskies.

THE PILLARS
9 Crichton Street
Tel: 01382 226278

Curiosity led us to The Pillars one night, and this is where the first seeds of this book were sown. We immediately took to the place and enjoyed the locals' banter and their friendliness towards these two strangers. We've been back a few times since, and on one occasion an extremely wobbly punter staggered over to us and asked if we were lesbians (two women drinking together – must be). It wasn't the least bit offensive though, just mildly funny – it's that kind of pub, one to become gradually fond of. The Pillars has the most peculiar layout, with the lounge bar 50 yards down the street, with its own front door. There's a long corridor at the back of the bar that will eventually lead you to the lounge; we recommend you take a packed lunch for the journey. The Pillars has lots of regulars, but it appeals to a mixed clientele, from old boys with their bags of messages enjoying an interim pint, to couples young and old, and the odd group of lads popping in for a bit of Saturday-night sanity. Two TVs are usually on, one of which is in an odd balcony setting, alongside a painting of the old Town House, and some large ceramic Laurel and Hardy figures. One of the framed pictures adorning the walls is an old whisky poster which looks as though it's been buried underground for a very long time. The beer selection is basic, with only cooking lager on tap, otherwise it's bottles. One of the remarkable things about The Pillars is that it's right in the middle of the city centre, but feels like a wee local tucked away somewhere. Look out for the stuffed pigeon nesting in the WW2 helmet on the shelf above the window.

RAT AND PARROT
85–87 Commercial Street
Tel: 01382 201042

This is the best of the large, lads'-night-out pubs in town. It really is very big, but despite leaning towards supermarket pub status, there is at least an attempt at ambience here. There are large comfortable sofas, wooden floors, antiquated birdcages, and a selection of framed art prints, such as Dufy and Matisse, in surprising blue frames, sitting a little uncomfortably alongside some peculiar mural 'remnants' featuring classical Roman or Grecian times – hard to distinguish. There's a reasonable selection of beer and lager and the usual spirits. The wine is basic, but it is bottled, which is a plus. This is generally a well-run pub and in good condition, fine for hen nights and leaving dos. Toilets are downstairs and require basic navigation skills.

STAR AND GARTER
42 Union Street
Tel: 01382 221366

Revisiting the Star and Garter after many years was a bit of a shock to the system. Green PVC, carpeted barstools, disturbingly ugly goblins and karaoke had replaced what I remember as earthy and traditional surroundings. Perhaps some pantomime disaster has turned all the old boys into goblins destined to hold pub lamps up for the rest of their days. The back room (or Saloon Bar) retains more of the original cosiness, with the old leaded windows and etched glass intact, despite attempts to upstage it with bright new furnishings. After initial misgivings and much bemoaning of 'why can't they leave places like this alone?', we realised that it's still essentially the same, in that it's a locals' pub with friendly, welcoming staff and cheery banter over the footie and boxing that are usually showing on the screen (when karaoke singers aren't following their bouncing ball up there). There seems to be an attempt to embrace the café culture that's taken over the city by introducing 'Essengees' – a funky take on 'S 'n' G' (Star and Garter) apparently. We did detect a couple of boxes of camomile and peppermint tea lurking behind the bar. Maybe 'Karaoke & Camomile' is the way forward, but I think it'll be a while before the rest of the world catches on to such a highly original concept. There's an average selection of ales, with Tennent's Velvet and Stella our choices of the day.

TAPAS BAR
16 Commercial Street
Tel: 01382 200527

When the Tapas Bar first opened, it was a real boon to the city, although we popped in one evening for a drink to find a couple of guys with guitars and sombreros serenading unassuming couples. I never saw this incident repeated, but did enjoy some great food here. At the time of writing, the Tapas Bar was closed down, the previous manager having fled back to Spain for one of many rumoured reasons.

Good news filtering through is that Jack Bruce, the driving force behind the once very fine Laings, has taken over, and it's due to reopen its savoury doors shortly. I, for one, am very much looking forward to the results.

TAY BAR
Dundee Railway Station

Let's face it, there's not a great deal to say about a bar in a railway station, but it's worth including for two reasons. Firstly, it's obviously very handy if you miss your train – although this will often be due to having spent too long in the pub in the first place. Another common occurrence is when you've gone to meet your beloved off their train which, when you get to the station, you discover has been delayed for any number of reasons, rarely disclosed to the humble passenger. If you know you're in for a bit of a wait, you may do well to head back over the walkway, and up to the Trades House Bar. If not, welcome to the Tay Bar. The second reason it deserves a mention is that they have three very fine original artworks on their walls. Okay, so three's not a very high number, but it's more original art than you'll see in most other pubs. One of these is a screen print by a very fine Scottish artist, Jim Pattison, a man I know 'waited for trains' in here on more than one occasion. You can even buy a Kit Kat at the bar, which makes a change from the pint/crisps pairing.

THOMSONS
66 Bell Street
Tel: 01382 205140

Despite its close proximity to Abertay University, Dundee High School, and not many houses, Thomsons manages to exist happily as a pleasant locals' pub. It's fairly basic, but is well cared for, a bit like an old faithful family dog who still gets a daily grooming. When I was there the service was very friendly and polite, and the immaculately dressed barman had a real sense of pride as he rearranged his nut display. The atmosphere was relaxed, with an amiable bunch of men chatting at the bar. This is the civilised end of men's pubs. Beer selection is average (80/-, Guinness), and there are six or seven decent malts displayed in the small but well-presented gantry, which is flanked on both sides by a couple of female torsos. The community spirit is echoed in the noticeboard, which informs of various events and domino competitions.

TICKETY BOOS
51 Commercial Street
Tel: 01382 227119

Despite having a name which no decent pub deserves (no self-respecting pub dog would accept such a name), Tickety Boos (herein known as TBs) is a fine wee pub. The staff were very friendly and helpful; the choice of beer and spirits was reasonable, although only draught wine was on offer. We were suitably refreshed with our respective pints of Stella and Tennent's Velvet. TBs attracts a healthy mix of clientele, including many regulars. There's a large-screen facility, presumably for sport, but mostly music is played – varied and unobtrusive. The noteworthy points of TBs are that they have a game show night (currently Thursday), and a quiz night, but no karaoke. Breakfast is served from 10 a.m. to noon, and in the summer months, or rather on warm days (not necessarily the same thing in Dundee), there is seating outside, although at times the number 32 bus comes a wee bit close for comfort. Generally, a good city-centre pub.

TOWN HOUSE
1 King Street
Tel: 01382 203311

This is *the* karaoke pub. If you don't like karaoke, stay away. However, if you do, you'll have a ball here. We visited one Thursday, when large groups of chums had congregated for the night and much dancing and singing was going on. It was a bit like accidentally gatecrashing a private party. Every table had the 'folder' open and serious karaoke kings and queens carefully chose who they were going to be tonight. I was disappointed to see there was no Shirley Bassey – not that I would have got up to sing – honest. Despite not being a fan of the Japanese singing sport, it's hard not to be affected by the good time that everyone else is having – although late in the evening, when one particular crooner got up to sing 'Country Roads', there seemed to be a mass exodus. The Town House specialises in karaoke discos. The décor is a bit lively for my taste, with orange gloss paint, and lots of red and gold everywhere, resulting in the birth of Butlins baroque. There are also curious paintings of old Dundee, but with people in contemporary dress.

This is obviously a well-run pub that knows its market and how to please its punters, which surely is a recipe for success. The atmosphere is very friendly and unpretentious, and it's a long time since I've seen such uninhibited dancing in the middle of a pub. Usual selection of McEwan's 80/- et al. Popular and busy at lunchtimes.

TRADES HOUSE BAR
40 Nethergate
Tel: 01382 229494

A relative newcomer to the Dundee pub scene, the Trades House Bar is a loving recreation of a Victorian-era pub. It's fitted out beautifully with oak; none of your veneer nonsense, this is the real thing and there's plenty of it. In fact, there's so much wood, you begin to wonder how many trees must have been involved – maybe not as many as it took to build the *Discovery*, but a pretty close second. All the fittings and furnishings were specially commissioned: the mosaic panels laid into the floor, the bespoke stained-glass windows which depict the trades of the city; even the pub mirrors are custom made. The interior design and specialist joinery work were undertaken by local firms, which fits in nicely with the Trades theme.

The bar staff will have you thinking you've gone back in time, decked out as they are in white shirts and ties, resplendent in their white pinnies; although the sudden appearance of a dreadlocked head soon snapped me back to the twenty-first century. The staff here are second to none. Not only are they friendly and knowledgeable, they take the trouble to remember your tipple, even if you haven't been in for a month. The long bar has a phenomenal selection of – well – just about anything you could wish for. Draught beers include Deuchars IPA (always a good sign in my book), Belhaven Best, St Andrews 80/-, as well as a fine choice of premium lagers, including Oranjeboom and Stella Artois. The gantry positively glitters with its countless bottles of everything imaginable.

The Trades is a big place, but the creation of three snug bars means you can enjoy a peaceful pint away from the main throng. Our favourite is the Nethergate Snug, perfect for the post-work pint, although there's only so many pint and crisp suppers a girl can take in a week . . .

The Morrison family have succeeded in producing a rarity here – a completely new pub in the middle of the town centre, which has become one of the best pubs around. A word of warning though: don't come on a Friday or Saturday night if it's conversation you're after. The Trades gets so busy they start queuing outside. We suggest going any other night of the week, when you can enjoy an air of city-centre calm.

YATES WINE LODGE
7–9 Seagate
Tel: 01382 227976

Another relatively new addition to the city-centre pub scene and not really a bonus. Yates is the very epitome of a chain pub. It is possibly the only pub in Dundee that gives you no indication of which city or country you're in. Soulless is an understatement. Thoroughly lacking in character, charm or any distinctive feature whatsoever is more accurate. There is, however, one attraction, which is not the 1980s bingo-hall-style décor, nor the size of the place (it is absolutely enormous, hence the popularity for stag/hen nights and so on). It is the absurdly cheap drink, possibly the cheapest in Dundee city centre. Cheap drink is great if you're short of a bob or two, but has its consequences, namely fights, throwing up (could explain the carpet) and serious serial drinking. Basically, it costs less to get plastered here. We went for our tea, which was poor to indifferent. It's a standard pub menu with everything sounding and looking like it's gone from freezer to microwave to table, and it is served accordingly. The bar service was okay, of that compulsory 'Have a nice day' variety; routine pleasantries rather than proper conversation. There is a more serious point to be made regarding the cheap chain pint. Yates is a large corporate venture that can afford low prices. Its popularity is at the expense of good local establishments which are frequently priced out of the market. It is the pub equivalent of a supermarket, and pub dog would be tied to a railing outside.

Perth Road and Nethergate

The Perth Road, leading down to Nethergate, is home to some of Dundee's finest pubs, and makes for a classic pub crawl. Whether you're working your way up from the Phoenix, or down from the Speedwell, you are guaranteed to start and finish your evening in a classic boozer.

ART BAR
140 Perth Road
Tel: 01382 227888

The name 'Art Bar' had me a bit sceptical; I was expecting some arty student haunt, but instead found a pleasant, laid-back basement bar. The general décor is stylishly basic, with an old stone floor, a fireplace, and one exposed stone wall. The other walls are painted a deep shade of red and are decorated with a series of digitally manipulated Old Masters. Being immediately opposite the art college, it's inevitable that students and staff will trickle through these doors, but it also attracts a whole bunch of other folk. It's easy to forget you're in Dundee in the Art Bar – not that you would want to do that, of course – and there's a cosmopolitan feel to the place, with jazz tunes in the bar, and classical music and opera playing in the toilets. There's nothing quite like peeing to Puccini. Most nights there's a live band – the place is tiny though, so stand well back from the zebra-print curtains when the two trumpeters take to the 'stage'. It's definitely more bar than pub, but does a decent pint of McEwan's 80/- and Kronenbourg on tap, and also bottles including Peroni and Budvar, all for less than most other arty joints charge. Due to the petite size of the Art Bar, it can get pretty smoky on a busy weekend, but it is a refreshing change for a mid-week tipple.

CUL DE SAC
10 South Tay Street
Tel: 01382 202070/227151

The Cul de Sac bar/café/restaurant is part of a small chain which started life in Glasgow. The Dundee version doesn't quite live up to the reputation of the originals, but is still a decent enough place to go. Despite being on street level, it feels like a basement bar, with its low ceiling, exposed stone, and wooden floor. Very low tables and big leathery settees and pouffes give it an informal, up-market-student-bedsit sort of air. It's all suitably stylish, popular with the young and trendy, with an in-house DJ spinning cool sounds on a weekend to get you into that club mood. Candles are a nice touch, enhancing the low-level lighting. The back part of the bar is quieter, with comfy booths and table football on the go. Hoegaarden, Stella, Boddingtons and Beamish Red are among the slightly pricey beer and lager. This is a popular pre-club venue, and a decent place for a mid-week, mellow pint.

The café/restaurant is situated beyond the bar, and also has its own entrance on Tay Square. The first time we visited, the staff screwed up our order. They did, to be fair, ply us with free wine, but by the time the correct meal was delivered, nearly an hour after we'd sat down, our empty stomachs had been filled with an extensive amount of it, and we probably didn't appreciate our food as much as we should have. It all seemed perfectly acceptable though, and fillet of red snapper, and pasta with spinach, mushroom and feta cheese were duly polished off. If you eat between 12 noon and 2 p.m., or 5 and 7 p.m., all crêpes, pasta and pizzas are half price, which is well worth sticking to these times for. We opted for crêpes – one with chickpeas, potatoes and green vegetables, which had a lovely subtle flavour (although it was a touch on the oily side) and a very palatable chicken, bacon and almond version. The crêpe itself was nicely browned, and the portion was just right for a healthy-sized lunch, but at full price it's on the small side. The mussels starter, however, was excellent value and came with a very good sauce. Other dishes included fillet or sirloin steaks, chicken stuffed with spinach and ricotta cheese, and a green-pepper-and-goat's-cheese filo pastry number. The main courses were fine, but the accompanying vegetables were very dull and uninspiring – a step up from school dinners. Pizzas were basic cheese-and-tomato, and you choose your own toppings. Sweets included Bailey's Irish Cream cheesecake and banana parfait. Service is variable, but generally good. The décor is fairly basic, with a wooden floor, and strong, dark colours on the walls. The back wall is decorated with a series of Polyfilla blobs which look as though they've been chucked from the other side of the room. At least they've been left white, unlike the ones outside, which have been painted jobby-brown, and do indeed look like big turds. Hardly an invitation to eat.

On the whole, the Cul de Sac serves up good, but not exceptional food, and is perfectly positioned in a part of town that's becoming increasingly popular with Dundee diners.

DCA
152 Nethergate
Tel: 01382 432281
(See review in 'Cafés' section.)

DROUTHY NEEBORS
142 Perth Road
Tel: 01382 202187

Formerly McGonagall's (and still called this by many) – the local bard has been traded in for the national one, as this is now part of the Drouthy Neebors chain which was named after a line in a Burns poem. The term 'chain pub' would usually fill us with dread, but we were pleasantly surprised here, as although it has a faux traditional look, they haven't gone overboard on the knick-knack front, preferring simply to put in wooden floors, tables, etc. There's also an unfortunate piece of mural painting produced by local art students above the tight spiral staircase which leads down to the loos. The downstairs bar is now 'd basement', a small venue for gigs and, at weekends, becomes a club. (See 'Live Music' section for more details.)

On the ale front, the choice is mainly Belhaven brews, with their Belhaven Best being very fine, and there are premium lagers such as Stella on offer. It's always been the second home for many art college students (and staff) but there's a healthy input of locals to keep the balance. We visited on a Saturday night when it was busy but not crowded, and the staff were very friendly and helpful. Food is served at lunchtime and early evening. There's a good eclectic selection of non-intrusive music on offer, and TVs which are mostly used for sporting occasions.

LAINGS BAR
8 Roseangle
Tel: 01382 221777

Under its previous owner, Jack Bruce, Laings was built up into something of an institution. Sadly for regulars, he sold up a few years ago, and the new version is a shadow of its former self. It still looks much the same, but there is one big change – the food. Whereas Laings of old was, quite literally, a legend in its own lunchtime, the food has now taken something of a back seat. The choice is more limited, and is generally not of the same calibre. They still sell a decent pint though, and one of its best features, the large beer garden, is still intact. Given that it's a bit of a trek down to it, the weather may have changed by the time you've spilt your way down the many steps. Best to take both sunglasses and brolly. If you don't feel like the walk, there is a covered decking area on the same level as the pub. Busiest during term time with both staff and students of nearby institutions.

NETHER INN
132 Nethergate
Tel: 01382 349970

This is one of those establishments which keeps changing its name/image/clientele every other year. At time of writing it's known as the Nether Inn (It's a Scream!) – one of the chain of 'Scream' pubs (so-called purely on the basis that each pub has an imitation of Munch's much maligned *The Scream* painting as part of its corporate identity). The main thing that struck us was the lack of choice of drink. Unless you're after brightly coloured liquid sweeties with alcohol, or a pint of After Shock, there's not much on offer. On asking what malts they had – come on, that's not an unreasonable request in a pub – we were informed that they only sell Bell's. So, no malts and only one blend. The clientele here are young, and mainly students, and it seems popular and always fairly lively. If you want a proper drink though, flee across the road to that safe house of taste, the Phoenix.

NOSEY PARKERS
Queens Hotel
Perth Road
Tel: 01382 322515

Nosey Parkers ('Come in and have a nosey' – must I?) is attached to the Queens Hotel, an imposing gothic building at the foot of the Perth Road. The hotel exterior is remarkable, akin to a spooky castle in a child's storybook, with turrets and the like. Its interior has a fusty fading grandeur, although changes seem to be afoot. Nosey Parkers is, however, something very different, an appalling concoction of ill-conceived themes. The comical name is dreadful, it actually makes me wince, like watching sex on TV when your parents are in the room. The interior is garish – not unlike the ante-room of a brothel, with its imitation animal-print furniture, although it never seems that busy. However, if you walk right through to the south-facing room, which is more akin to a children's nursery, you'll find they cook up some tasty fare. I've not sampled it personally, but good reports have come in from reliable sources. I have to say though, that to have fajitas spelt out phonetically as 'fa-hee-tas' is ever so slightly condescending. Eating here is not to be confused with eating in the Queens Hotel itself, however. The vegetarian option on their 2000 Christmas menu was a bean salad. We phoned the Queens and suggested that maybe this wasn't very festive, what with it being December, and the Lord's birthday and all that. Friends of ours were unfortunate enough to go for their work's Christmas night out in the lower function room, and the reports were *not* good. They did change the bean salad into a lasagne though, so there's something. Nosey Parkers has live jazz on a Sunday afternoon which draws a bit of a crowd.

PHOENIX BAR
103 Nethergate
Tel: 01382 200014

Hooray for the Phoenix. It is owned by the highly entertaining Alan Bannerman (or Mr Phoenix as we call him) who is so at home behind his bar, it's a pity he's not there more often, although his excellent team of friendly bar staff will make you feel quite at home. For me, the Phoenix just has everything you could want in a pub. Its closeness to the city centre allows non-Westenders to visit a favourite pub without having to trek up the Perth Road or hop on the Broughty Ferry bus. The quality and choice of beer has to be some of the best in town; their Deuchars IPA is a dream pint – every time. There are always guest beers as well as the regulars, including the aforementioned Deuchars, McEwan's 80/-, Orkney Island, Hoegaarden, Kronenbourg and Guinness. They also have a very fine selection of whiskies and an abundance of rums, amongst other spirits.

The Phoenix isn't a well-preserved gem, or an earthy bare-bones kind of a place, but it genuinely enjoys being a pub. The atmosphere is so comfortable, you really feel at home here. Its rich reds and dark wood add to the warmth, and the seating areas allow an amount of privacy, with leaded glass panels between each one. If you find yourself seated on one of the throne-like chairs, you'll rightly feel like a pub king or queen; two chairs are particularly enormous and take a skilled hand to manoeuvre safely. The walls are bedecked with a great selection of old local signs. Some favourites of mine are: 'Cock Sole Leather', 'Redferns for Rubbers', and the 'General Office and Enquiries' sign above the door of the gents toilet. There's also a very large collection of beer mats, and a stag's head with a lit sign for 'Schlitz', which somehow fits perfectly between its antlers. For added entertainment, there are two TVs (with sound rarely up), and unobtrusive and well-chosen music (Van Morrison, Bob Dylan, jazz, soul, etc).

Into the bargain, they also serve great pub food. Their steak sandwich is reputed to be exceptional, and the chunky pizzas can be divvied up between two. You may be confused by the symbol which pops up next to anything chilliesque in nature, which states that it 'denotes the start of *Bonanza*'. (Just think about the burning hole as the opening credits roll. We were told the full story, with extra relish. If you want to know, you'll have to ask Mr Phoenix yourself.) Highly recommended.

Contrary to popular belief, the Phoenix was never called Fenwick's. It was, however, once owned by a couple called the Fenwicks. This situation has resulted in much confusion, as presumably, for a spell, the pub was referred to as Fenwick's rather than Phoenix. It did go through a short period in the '80s with the unfortunate name of 'The Town and Gown'.

Legend has it that Frank Sinatra once drank in the Phoenix Bar. He'd played a gig at the Caird Hall (this much is definitely true), which wasn't that well attended, and he invited the audience to sit at the front, which didn't please the folk who'd paid more for their tickets. Whether he was drowning his sorrows over this fall in popularity, or the fact that he'd not long split up with Ava Gardner, isn't clear, but if a pint in the Phoenix is good enough for old Frankie boy, it's good enough for us.

POPL NERO
141 Perth Road
Tel: 01382 226103

The thing that struck me most in Popl Nero was the impressive selection of spirits and liqueurs. They don't use optics, so all are stacked on tiered wooden shelves, and look quite splendid. There must be about ten types of Absinthe alone, as well as a whole bunch of stuff I'd never heard of, and couldn't pronounce anyway. Polish rather than Russian vodka seems to be the main choice. Pints on offer include Calders 80/-, Calders Cream, Guinness and Stella. Coffee is on all day, so if you've had one too many shots of Mescal, you can level out with a cappuccino, even at 11 p.m.

Popl Nero is quite a modern, trendy kind of bar, but has been designed with some thought. The space is surprisingly homely, with big wooden 'kitchen' tables, some slightly tatty leather chairs, and a couple of settees for relaxing. The colour scheme is very earthy, with warm terracottas and ochres, and feels a bit like a Spanish tavern. The chunky wooden beams, which are used throughout, are a nice touch. Look out for the high-pressure – and highly individual – beer pumps which make for a talking point at the bar (is the beer here really that strong?). There is a large student clientele, but not exclusively so. It's a popular spot for afternoon lounging, although the music levels vary and can be a bit loud at times for relaxing conversation. There is also a large screen showing unidentifiable footage.

We popped in once for coffee and got great service, encouraging us to revisit for lunch the following week. Sadly, this was a different story altogether, involving yet another order cock-up for us, but without the usual goodwill gesture of free drinks or even a genuine apology. This was a one-off, but the service was decidedly sloppy, and it showed up a serious inconsistency with the staff. It's always a pity when someone lets the side down. Other than this blip, we liked the easy-going atmosphere of Popl Nero. Weekends see it in full swing with pre-clubbers, but it's a good stop for a mellow mid-week pint, or afternoon cuppa.

RAFFLES
18 Perth Road
Tel: 01382 226344

Raffles isn't great at being either a café or a bar, although given its popularity on a weekend it obviously has more success at the latter. There are great views over the River Tay and the railway bridge and a pleasant atmosphere on a Sunday, when they serve breakfast (including a vegetarian option) with appropriately lazy music. The food (ordered at the bar) is standard fare: burgers, stuffed tortillas, panini breads, fish and chips, lasagne – not really of notable quality. We've heard varied reports of the food here, some good, some bad, so the fairest we can say is that it's reliably inconsistent. Raffles is a very different place on an evening; it has loud music and is popular with students and, at weekends, pre-clubbers. It's all a far cry from the lacy curtains and to-die-for hot chocolate from my student days in the old Raffles. More suited to a party dog than a pub dog.

SPEEDWELL BAR/MENNIES
165–167 Perth Road
Tel: 01382 667783

Much praise has been heaped on this absolute legend of a pub, and understandably so. It does, however, make it a little daunting to write about such a place. One of the first things to mention is its two names. It's officially called the Speedwell Bar, but having been in the hands of a Mrs, or 'Ma', Mennie for over half a century, it's still known by many as Mennies. This can cause a bit of confusion for newcomers, but you'll get used to it. Another of Dundee's institutions which has found its way into the safe hands of Jonathan Stewart, it now, not surprisingly, features regularly in the *CAMRA Good Beer Guide*. It's famed, and now listed, for its spectacular interior which has been beautifully preserved, and sports many notable features. The mahogany bar, gantry, panelling and fireplaces – the etched-glass screens and windows – and I've heard the gents toilets are noteworthy, with all the original fittings still in place, the old high-sided urinals giving a privacy otherwise unheard of in the world of men's loos (so I'm told). Unfortunately, the ladies' loos were never given the same treatment, although they do have a nice wee bit of mosaic floor. Despite all this awe-inspiring Victorian splendour, it's not a pub simply for 'sightseeing', and it is thoughtfully, rather than preciously, preserved. It's a true drinkers' pub, and there's much evidence of a century of good drinking, with suitably worn and scuffed fittings adding to the charm.

The layout of the Speedwell is unusual. The main bar is L-shaped, with a very long counter, and is partly divided by a low, glazed screen. The main area has no tables, just some stools along the length of the bar. Instead, there are two panelled rooms, which are to the left of the bar, now designated as smoking and non-smoking. The first of these is the more basic, with an almost rusty-looking lino floor, and simple chairs and tables. A very high PVC window seat/bench runs the full length of one wall, and it made me feel about eight years old, with my wee legs dangling mid-air. The back room, divided from the first by a wood/glazed partition, is the no-smoking room. This is more like a lounge bar, with more upmarket furnishings, and is a welcome retreat for those averse to a smoky Saturday-night atmosphere, as it's quite self-contained. With a diverse bunch of customers, Mennies is a busy pub, but rarely heaving and, strangely, you can nearly always get a seat. They serve up a great selection of some of the finest beer in town, with Deuchars IPA and St Andrews 80/- among the stars. They also have an amazing selection of whiskies; I tried to count them, unsuccessfully, but I can say fairly that there are well over 100. You can even call in for coffee, and you are welcome to bring your own baking from the next-door bakers, Goodfellow and Steven. What better surroundings to eat an individual fruit pie? Speedwell/Mennies doesn't really need anyone to sing its praises, but if you've never been here before, I heartily recommend that you change your ways.

TAVERN BAR
168 Perth Road
Tel: 01382 227135

The Tavern is a fairly solid, traditional pub. Despite its close proximity to the art college and university, it's not overrun with students, and a good mix of folk enjoy a pint here. The deep-red leathery seating is virtually continuous throughout the main part of the pub, with no partitions interrupting it. This is great for large groups, and is conducive to a very social drinking atmosphere, although the separate tables mean that you can feel equally content in small bunches. I thought this kind of large seating expanse was quite unusual, but a fellow drinker insisted that there's a pub in Kelty with a similar layout. So, not unusual at all then, if you're an ex-miner from Fife.

The décor is generally unremarkable, although on a recent visit it didn't escape my notice that the lower parts of the walls and the radiators had been given a coat of mint-green paint. I can only hope that this is a passing experiment, and that sombre tones will be put back in place. Wooden beams above the bar are complemented by a curious central fan feature set into the ceiling. Another popular pub for sporty viewing, I recall a very special evening during the 1990 World Cup, when the 'Tav' was brought alive by Cameroonians, Africans and Scots all cheering on the Cameroons as they faced the favoured England side. It was a fantastic game, ending in a 3–3 draw. Sadly, the underdogs lost out on a penalty shoot-out, but not before some serious partying had gone on. This is an unpretentious pub where, given the chance, pub dog would happily drink Guinness from one of their ashtrays.

TAYBRIDGE BAR
129 Perth Road
Tel: 01382 643973

One of Dundee's legendary pubs, the Taybridge first opened its doors to the Dundee drinker in 1876, and although it may not be as old as the hills, it is as old as the bridge. It's split into three different bars – the Bar, the Walnut Lounge, and the Lounge. A tiny snug, marginally larger than the Tardis, with its own door, is on your left as you enter the main bar. The bar is where the real drinking gets done and is a bare-bones affair, with a slightly sparkly, industrial floor. The décor has remained virtually unchanged over the years, and behind the bar it boasts its original gantry and a beautiful etched mirror with a view of the Tay Bridge. Aside from some bar stools – and a wee raised area at the back with a couple of tables, a small library, and some curious drawings of ex-footballers – the bar is standing-room only. Although it has a reputation as a man's bar, I've never felt out of place in here and prefer it to the more 'comfortable' lounge, where pop music is piped out, in contrast to the music-free policy of the bar. They do have one TV in the bar, mainly for football games. We were in one Sunday afternoon, and a tray of delicious home-made soup came round; a rare and welcome kind of hospitality these days. This would have been the perfect place for pub dog to enjoy an ashtray of 80/-, but sadly, apart from guide-dogs, the Taybridge is now a dog-free zone. They used to allow them in, but apparently there were sometimes so many dogs in the pub that fights would inevitably break out, so they were all barred (a policy which many other pubs would do well to enforce on their punters). The Walnut Lounge gets its name from its walnutty finish. The entire space is panelled in walnut veneer, and is wholly art deco, with some wonderful deco-etched glass – worth popping in to see. The larger lounge is the area that has changed the most. My earliest recollection of the lounge is of a kind of chair cemetery for large orange armchairs. I seem to remember you could hardly move for the things, although it *was* a long time ago, and, well – my memory . . . It's had a couple of facelifts since then, the current one is more traditional. The corridor that links the bar and the lounge has a number of old and new images of the Tay Bridge, which are worth a look. Back to the bar though for a decent pint. I have it on good authority that the 80/- in the bar is far superior to that in the lounge. Strange, but true. The Taybridge is a lovely old pub, and is a great place to sup a few delicious pints. A popular regulars' pub, and rightly so.

The Taybridge Bar is the setting for a Michael Marra song, 'Frida Kahlo's Visit to the Taybridge Bar', from his album Posted Sober. *The song also mentions a very fine Dundee painter, Jimmy Howie, who is also one of Dundee's greatest dancers; I've witnessed his grace and style on many occasions at the Coffee Bar disco at the Art College, amongst other places. It was only a matter of time before his talents would find their place in one of Michael's songs. Anyone who has seen this extraordinary sight will fully understand why, on being sent by Saint Peter to the Taybridge Bar – 'She said, "Put on Perdido, tonight's the night, I want to dance with Jimmy Howie in the pale moonlight."'*

Hawkhill and Westport

BALGAYHILL BAR
1–3 Rosefield Street (bar entrance on Blackness Road)
Tel: 01382 668921

Not really Hawkhill *or* Westport, but I'd always thought this looked like a fine old pub from the outside, so fancied paying it a visit. It is indeed a lovely traditional pub, the bar being particularly to my liking, with its suitably well-trodden lino floor. There are brass rails along the top and bottom of the bar itself, old tiles which also continue round the walls, and proper radiators which are perfect for leaning against on a cold night. The main seating area is in a large alcove, but most folk seem to prefer to stand. The bar has a good, warm atmosphere, and has lots of regular customers. There's a television, but no music, and a decent selection of Tennent's Velvet, 80/-, Caffrey's, Guinness and Grolsch on tap, and fine pints were had by all the night we were there.

The lounge, which you can enter from Rosefield Street, has quite a different feel. Music is played here, and the look is less individual than the bar. It still has a good locals' atmosphere though. If you've traipsed up to Mills Observatory on Balgay Hill, this might just be the perfect place to warm your telescope on the way home.

CAMPBELTOWN BAR
271 Hawkhill
Tel: 01382 668251

This is one of Dundee's oldest pubs, and is a gloriously unpretentious wee place. It really is quite small, and as you step over the threshold, which is made up of salvaged railway line from the first Tay Bridge, and enter the 'Cammie', you will find one of Dundee's tiniest snugs immediately on your left. This is a proper postage-stamp-sized snug, which only seats four, so if it's full, you can seat yourself in the cosy corner by the window or at one of the two very small tables on either side of the fireplace. The Cammie is popular with bowlers, although in-house sport seems to be restricted to dominoes. A special wooden table top gets brought out for this – more likely because the tables are so wee, rather than to protect their surface.

A few short steps lead you up to the loos and the lounge, which has the feel of an old living-room. The Campbeltown is a great wee pub, full of character and characters. Even the ancient red lino floor looks as though it could tell a few stories of its own. Joyfully, there's no music and just one TV, mainly for watching sport. I've nothing against pubs that do food, but it cheers me that pubs like the Campbeltown haven't felt the need to go down this road, and exist very happily as what they truly are – drinking houses. They do serve the odd hot pie, but that goes with the territory. They also serve a lovely pint of Belhaven Best, among the expected choices. A wee gem, and a pub dog favourite.

An extract from Bill Duncan's *Smiling School For Calvinists* (Bloomsbury Publishing):

'On Leaving a Volume of Søren Kierkegaard's *Fear and Trembling* in the Back Room of the Campbeltown Bar, Dundee.'

Returning ten minutes later, scanning my now occupied seat I feign composure and approach the bar.

'Donald, did anybody hand in a book?'

'Aye.'

He reaches under the counter. I try to avoid the stares of the front room as he looks at the back cover, frowns, looks at the front cover where Søren Kierkegaard glowers back at him.

He stares at me, hands me the book and is about to say something when a voice asserts:

'Crisps? A dear fuckin wey o' eatin a tattie.'

THE DOGHOUSE
13 Brown Street
Tel: 01382 227080

This was originally converted from an old schoolhouse into a pub by the Firkin chain (Dundee, being famous for its journalistic output, led to it being named the Freelance and Firkin). It never really worked, and it always felt a bit like sitting in a warehouse. The new owners have improved on this greatly, with the space now occasionally being split into two. In the bar itself, there are big leathery settees and an old-looking wooden floor, giving the place a comfy, relaxed feel. The Doghouse used to play host to Dundee's only comedy club, attracting names such as Michael Redmond and Phil Kay. However, recent reports tell me the comedy club is moving to the Dundee Rep. The Doghouse is also used as a music venue (see 'Live Music' section for details). The Doghouse is one of the few pubs in town to have a pool room. It's also noteworthy for having a late-night café, which is open from 11 p.m. to 4 a.m., serving full cooked breakfasts (including a veggie one), as well as burgers, waffles, and a whole host of other three-in-the-morning requirements, with coffee and soft drinks, but no alcohol. Outside The Doghouse, there's a 'What's On' chalkboard, with a listing of the forthcoming week's events. Currently, a typical week will include everything from a live band to an afternoon tea dance and a quiz and karaoke night – something for everyone. They also have their own excellent website which will give you all the info you need to know about forthcoming gigs and comedy events here, as well as its full menu (daytime and nocturnal). There's an average to good selection of beers and spirits and a fairly basic beer garden, which is popular on sunny days, but not exactly in an idyllic spot, being right next to the busy Hawkhill.

GLOBE BAR
53–57 West Port
Tel: 01382 224712

Despite being a grand old building with a good interior, for us this was the least memorable of the pubs in this area. Obviously once a fine old establishment, it seems to have lost interest in being a pub, which is a pity, as it could be great. Granted, it was extremely quiet when we visited, and it's highly probable that come the weekend, things liven up here, certainly during term time. Unfortunately, the choice of beer and lager is poor, and the wine is on draught. It's a sign of the times when a decent pint is replaced with vodka jelly, and bottles of Hooch for a pound. One suspects there is possibly more action in the loos, with a 'Naughty Sex Machine' selling pheromone wipes, edible undies, handcuffs, etc. Music policy is dance-based, which is great in some venues, but in a large, virtually empty space, it just doesn't work. It did get a bit more lively after 10.30 p.m., and I hear it's popular for eats at lunchtime.

HAWKHILL TAVERN
247 Hawkhill
Tel: 01382 668800

We visited this pub on two very different occasions: one was an afternoon when it was jam-packed with footie fans watching Scotland versus England (the score? Oh, er, I can't remember . . .) and the other on a quiet Tuesday evening. Both were thoroughly enjoyable experiences. It's the sign of a fine pub to be able to embrace such diversity so effortlessly. The staff are extremely friendly and attentive; the clientele a healthy blend of locals and beyond – those seeking a proper pub in the wilderness? Well, not quite, but since the sad demise of the original Hawkhill, the Tavern and its neighbour, the Campbeltown, are like gems in the black-ness. It's an extremely well-stocked bar and has a wonderful display of shelf upon shelf of inviting bottles. Pretty much anything you care to ask for is here somewhere. There are many fine malts in attendance too. Walking through the doors of the Hawkhill Tavern, you immediately feel very welcome, and for my money that's worth its weight.

MEZZO BAR
2 West Port
Tel: 01382 225285

Probably best known to most as 'The Ascot', this ill-fated corner site seems to have trouble creating a success story. Currently operating as the Mezzo café bar, it's presumably somewhere you might like to stop off for a coffee of an afternoon. We popped in on a Saturday night around 9 p.m. when most of its neighbours were stowed out. It's one thing looking for a quiet drink, but the Mezzo was barely whispering. An attempt to heighten the atmosphere involved *Who Wants To Be A Millionaire?* blasting out from the TV. The two barmaids added to the ambience by sharing a Chinese carryout at the end of the bar. It seems a little busier during the day for coffee and sandwiches.

MICKEY COYLE'S
21–23 Old Hawkhill
Tel: 01382 225871

This is a friendly, lively pub, and by far the most pleasant in this stretch of publand. It's rather like being in a big living-room, with generally eclectic décor that seems to reflect the interests of its patrons and staff. It can be fairly loud, but it's a good-spirited atmosphere, with a happy mixture of locals and students. A popular pub quiz takes place once a week, and is always good fun. Despite earlier mutterings about music in pubs, MC's plays music quite loudly, but it works here, probably because they play a genuinely good, varied selection of sounds which suit the atmosphere, rather than trying to create it. A local band, The Mudskippers, play once a week. It's busy at lunchtime with hungry university staff and local business types – and these visits sometimes stretch to teatime. Basic pub food is served, which is of decent quality, and there are bargain rates through the week. The baked tatties are properly baked and not microwaved, which is always appreciated. There is also a wine-and-cheese platter for a tenner. Forthcoming events, extras on the menu, special offers and so on are chalked up on proper blackboards, and not those terrible faux painted blackboards that you see everywhere these days. MC's keeps an excellent selection of beer, with beauties such as Deuchars IPA, Caledonian 80/- and Belhaven Best permanently on offer. You'll also find the perfect host in Scotty, who many will remember from his days in the Westport Bar.

PIVO BAR
1 Temple Lane
Tel: 01382 223095

Part of a small chain, this is a welcome newcomer to the Westport gang. It's based on a Czech theme, although it bears no resemblance to any pubs I visited in Prague – and I saw the inside of a fair few. The interior is refreshingly simple and uncluttered, with a couple of long wooden tables with benches, which are long enough to seat eight, or to spread out your broadsheet. There are also some smaller chunky tables, with great wee stools which look like vaulting horses for dwarfs. It's all very comfy and stylish. The lighting is subtle, with some curious '60s sci-fi-style wall lamps. The beer obviously deserves a mention, with two Czech beers on draught, including Staropramen, and a good choice in bottles. The best known, and very fine Budvar is here too, but it's worth sampling some of the less pronounceable ones, in particular the Krusovice Royal Black, a prince of beers, which is a delicious, dark, non-gassy lager, if you can imagine such a thing. Highly recommended. There's also Gambrinus, and Krusovice Light, a strong, blond cousin of the royal one. They also sell coffee, reasonably priced sandwiches, and a touch of Czech goulash, though thankfully without the dumplings. Pivo gets busy and noisy at weekends, with a menu of guest DJs lining up to spin their *deskas*. Also, it's the official pre-club pub for the nearby club, Oxygen. A mellow pint can be enjoyed on a week night. Just be sure you know your *Pani* from your *Damy*. Oh, and in case you're wondering, *pivo* is Czech for beer.

ROYAL OAK
167 Brook Street
Tel: 01382 229440
(See 'Where to Eat' section.)

TALLY HO
11–13 Old Hawkhill
Tel: 01382 228500

This is positioned between Mickey Coyle's and The Globe – both geographically and in pub quality. It's a very average pub, although the staff are friendly. Popular mainly with students, it serves pitchers of cocktails and an average selection of beers. They also have a 'vodka bar' which was closed when we visited. There is a pull-down screen, presumably for sporting events, plus a couple of TVs showing MTV. The décor is oddly lacking – in so much as it's not really there, aside from a pseudo brick wall that resembles Jack and Vera's but without the added interest of the blue and yellow paint. Essentially, it's a large bar, good for student nights out with lots of folk in tow, but otherwise lacking in character or characters (I'm sure the Duckworths could soon change that). Two very good things that the Tally Ho has going for it are the real fire – for which they earn their brownie points – and a beer garden. Good to see they're providing for all seasons.

WESTPORT BAR
22 East Henderson's Wynd
Tel: 01382 200993

Well established, well loved, and, like a favourite teddy bear, well worn. This cosy corner of a pub, affectionately known as 'the Westie', may have changed hands over the years, but no one has ever felt the need to change the heart of the pub. It's a fairly basic wee place with an average choice of beers and spirits, but the friendliness and relaxed feel of the Westie more than makes up for that. A good eclectic selection of music is played, and there's a TV and a pull-down large screen for those vital sporting events (mainly footie). Upstairs, the Westie branches out into a music venue – it's not very big, but it attracts the names. Dundee's finest, Michael Marra, has played here on many occasions and it's always heaving. For a man who can fill much, much larger venues outside his home city, it's a tribute to the man, and indeed to the Westie, that he chooses to play to his loyal Dundee fans in this 'intimate' venue. There are bands here most nights of the week (see 'Live Music' for details). The most outstanding feature of the Westie is its food, which has to be in the top three of pub food available in Dundee. The menu is excellent, the prices reasonable, and when the food arrives you are not disappointed. My curry, made with fresh, imaginative vegetables, and served with basmati rice and naan bread, was a pleasant change from what is often served in 'higher class' restaurants. We like this pub.

East End and Hilltown

BALMORE BAR
47 Dura Street
Tel: 01382 453992

I've always had a soft spot for the Balmore. Although I've never had what I would call a local up this end of town, if any pub were to come close, it would have to be the Balmore. In an area that has become the land of used goods, rather than the land o' cakes, the Balmore is a wee gem. Very much a locals' place, in the true sense, it's a long-established and largely unspoiled traditional pub with gorgeous old buckled, almost melting, stained-glass leaded windows (now protected from the elements), and some lovely old wood and brass features, including a brass footrail around the bar, which pub dog would happily lean against whilst asleep on the well-trodden lino floor. Darts and dominoes feature prominently in the Balmore activities scene, with a proper wee chalk board for your 180s to be recorded on. They even have a cabinet in which to display the spoils of the success of the darts and dominoes teams. There's no music, but there are two TVs which purr away quietly in the background. Staff for the most part are friendly. There's also a modernised lounge to the rear with a juke box, but for character and atmosphere, stick to the bar. There's an average selection of beers, but what it does serve is an above-average pint at a below-average price. Well worth a visit.

BENSONS
4–6 Arbroath Road
Tel: 01382 453730

The thing I used to like about Bensons was the fact that the bar took its name from the butler in the wonderful TV series *Soap* (the one where a young Billy Crystal played a gay ventriloquist, and Burt was taken over by an alien . . . ?). The family butler was called Benson, who went on to get his own spin-off series, simply called *Benson*. To illustrate the connection, there were, at most, around six photographs of Benson around the pub. Tongue-in-cheek? Perhaps not, but it did have a certain quirkiness. Although it's still called Bensons, the photos are no longer there, and given that these were the main attraction, it's kind of lost its charm. A fairly ordinary boozer, brightly lit, with a very small bar, it has its fair share of regulars, although a much younger bunch than in the days of the butler.

BOWBRIDGE BAR
2 Main Street
Tel: 01382 810450

Like many pubs in the area, the Saturday afternoon match atmosphere is quite different from a mid-week one. Being a footie themed pub, it was no surprise to find the bar heaving with men on a Saturday afternoon, and the level of pub swearing was the most consistent and voluminous we have ever heard. We retreated, reluctantly, to the lounge which resembled the bad living-room of a modern bungalow. In retrospect, it was probably the wrong place to enter into a discussion about the differences between diphthongs and triphthongs.

Revisiting mid-week, we experienced a more mixed clientele (including a couple of women), mostly watching one of three strategically placed TVs. *The National Television Awards* happened to be on, which provided great entertainment, more because of the running commentary in the bar. One old boy seemed so carried away that he kept losing his false teeth. The Bowbridge is a surprisingly large pub for its location. The décor is plain, with no exceptional features, other than the framed Dundee and Dundee United strips (encouraging to see equal support for both sides), and some old black-and-white football team photos. We were made to feel welcome enough, and noted that the phenomenal levels of swearing are reserved for Saturdays.

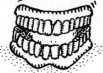

CLEP BAR
96–98 Clepington Road
Tel: 01382 858953

A priceless gem, and another Dundee legend. Many accolades have been showered on the Clep, and rightly so. Built as a working man's pub in the 1940s, it not only continues to fulfil its original purpose, it remains utterly intact. Reputedly Dundee's first scheme pub, and now a listed building, its interior is second to none. The original sign outside, the stained glass, the simple curves of the leather and wood seating, the wood panelled walls and chequered lino floor are all as they were. The feeling of having gone back in time was further enhanced on a recent visit, when *The Sweeney* and *Dukes of Hazzard* were showing on the telly – it seemed very apt somehow. This place is still popular for a post-work, pre-tea pint and is arrived at sometimes with so much eagerness, that a pencil still propped behind an ear is not an uncommon sight. The teatime rush seemed to happen between 4.30 p.m. and 5 p.m., which is very civilised. The walls are adorned with some visual treats, such as fascinating sporting photographs, a variety of old brewery mirrors, a fine collection of coshes behind the bar (one of which looks as if it belonged to the Slag Brothers from *Wacky Races*), and some policemen's whistles and handcuffs. Also, the original museum-worthy pre-decimal cash register still sits behind the bar.

The Clep is possibly the only pub in Dundee to still have a Jug Bar, for the original beer carry-out. A popular pub for pre- and post-match pints, it was once so stowed out that pals of ours were ushered into this tiny cupboard-sized space, as there was literally nowhere else to put them. An intimate experience, I believe.

My first-ever drink in the Clep was at a time when women weren't allowed in the bar. This would have been unacceptable to us in any other pub, but somehow in the Clep, you didn't mind. We drank instead in the very fine lounge, where table service is the order of the day and each table is equipped with its own bell. What better way to have your superior pint of McEwan's 80/- served than by a cheery barman in a long white apron bringing it to your table? They even come back with your change.

The Clep is a simple pub, but has such

style that it rises far above your average boozer. Thankfully it's far enough out of town not to be spoilt by suits and pseuds.

FREW'S BAR
117 Strathmartine Road
Tel: 01382 810975

Situated at a corner of the world known as Coldside, Frew's is here to warm your cockles. Although the huge fireplace was fireless when we visited, given the size of the guard around it, they must have some absolute blazers here. It's a fine-looking Victorian pub, full of original features. The gantry is panelled with a series of bevelled-edged mirrors which seem to give the bar an extra dimension – but this may have simply been the effects of the very fine Caledonian 80/- we were treated to. We particularly liked the floor, which was like a big tartan carpet, only more subtle, and was made from lino – lovely old lino that you can't replace, so I hope they don't. The only problem I had with the décor was the decision to paint the ceiling in a deep salmon pink, and to fix an incongruously modern paper border below it. I would suggest a tone more akin to 'dusty trombone', which would fit in well with the instrument collection above the bar.

Frew's has a very comfortable feel to it. The staff are friendly, and as well as being a great locals' pub, it's also popular for a pre- and post-match pint.

HALLEY'S BAR
22 Strathmartine Road
Tel: 01382 810440

A great watering-hole in the Hilltown desert, and worth the slog up the hill. If you need a breather on the way, I've always found the stunning St Salvador's church a worthwhile diversion. Halley's is a classic old boozer that had some major redécoration a number of years ago, but still retains a traditional feel, an impressively high nicotine-stained ceiling, and a great atmosphere. Given its relative proximity to Tannadice and Dens, Halley's is popular for a pre- and post-match pint, and even when it's heaving with supporters from both sides, it always manages to retain an air of civility. Similarly, on a Saturday night, there's a very amiable atmosphere, with a happy mix of folk, and good crack all round. What's more, one of the cheery barmen will pour you a fine, cheap pint of McEwan's 80/- which is definitely worth the Hilltown mountaineering challenge. They also serve 70/-, Guinness, and a selection of old-school bottles, including Sweetheart Stout and McEwan's Export, with Beck's bucking the trend for the more modern drinker, all of which is just fine with me. There's one TV, on which sport channels are given absolute priority, a couple of gaming machines, and no music. The walls are minimally garnished with a few sepia photos of the old trams, and an odd bunch of witches hang out behind the bar. (No, not the staff.) For a bit more privacy, there's a good-sized snug to your left which has a sliding door with a wee porthole in it. This neat and tidy old pub is a polished gem amidst a sea of rough diamonds.

JUNCTION BAR
9–11 Victoria Street
Tel: 01382 451292

Worth a mention for its doorbells alone. Not the fanciest of pubs, it does however have a certain quirkiness. Perhaps it's the pub sign – some time ago the 'J' fell off, and for many months the pub was fondly known as the 'Unction'. A 'J' has now been fashioned from an old scrap of plywood but looks like a back-to-front 'L', so is now called the 'Lunction'. By us anyway. (It was at one time called the Toby Jug after the owner's dog, Toby Joe.)

We were here once when there was a power cut

but we were all supplied with candles to carry on our evening. We were even given one to take to the toilet, which was interesting (just watch out for that dripping wax . . .). Each table in the lounge has its own bell for table service. These are doorbells with slightly different timbres (well, different ding-dongs). The J/U/Lunction is a bit dilapidated and basic, but not without charm. Unpretentious. Oh, and they serve beer.

LADYWELL
16 Victoria Road
Tel: 01382 223586

The Ladywell and I go back many years. When I first started drinking here, it not only had a wee back room, it also had a snug lounge which had a separate entrance from the bar. Me and my chum used to come here for a weekly watering after an art class, and one night we had a whole bag of paintbrushes destroyed when an old man sat on them. The snug and the brushes are long gone, and the Ladywell has undergone many facelifts over the years. It did, however, come as a bit of a shock on a recent visit to discover the wee back room also gone. This was where we always sat after a night at the Steps Cinema (pre-DCA days). The good-humoured barman and customers suggested I must be about 60 to remember all this. The atmosphere is relaxed and boyish, and you can order a toastie at the bar to accompany you through the latest footie game on the two TVs. The Ladywell went through a karaoke phase a few years back, but I think they've got over it, and it now seems to be a music-free zone. They serve up an above-average pint, including Belhaven on draught, and cheery banter. They have kept the open fire, which is great, and despite the changes it's still a decent pub. It's just a bit sad that so many well-loved old boozers have done themselves up as traditional pubs, when they had all the original ingredients to begin with.

ROSS'S BAR
85 Arbroath Road

This pub is nothing special to look at, reminiscent as it is of your old spinster auntie's very plain living-room. It is, however, a beacon of friendliness on a long pub-less stretch of road, and when we visited it was a bit like being at a happy family gathering (now there's a rarity). The other good thing was the jukebox, which had a surprisingly broad selection of tunes, from Neil Young to Neil Diamond, the Rolling Stones to Abba, and Serge Gainsbourg to the Verve. It's bit dearer than other east end pubs we've visited, but the well-poured McEwan's 80/- was more than palatable. One customer seemed overly concerned about his friend not making it to the chipper in time, with repeated refrains of 'aye, ye'll no' be gettin' yer fish supper the night, Irene!' echoing around the bar. Bless.

SHAKESPEARE BAR
267 Hilltown
Tel: 01382 225797

The Shakespeare – or 'Shakey' as it's affectionately known – was at one time owned by the estimable Jonathan Stewart, when it was, understandably, a bastion of very fine ales. He won the Publican of the Decade when in residence here. Some time has passed, and the Shakey is now a purveyor of average ales, and the bar and lounge have been knocked into one. It's a locals' pub where most folk know each other, and is best described as 'frisky'. A minor fight kicked off when we visited which went along the lines of 'Put him down, Kenny, he's an old man.' Kenny did eventually put him down and was duly scolded by the plucky barmaid. It doesn't quite match the standards set by the

Bowbridge for Saturday swearing, but it's a close second. We liked the sign at the bar which reads 'If you want a sub, ask the navy, not Sandy'. To remind you where you are, a picture of the Bard himself takes centre stage behind the bar.

SNUG BAR
75 Church Street
Tel: 01382 226978

A popular pre- and post-match pub with the Tangerines. We visited on the unfortunate occasion of a league match twixt United and Rangers, when, despite being 1–1 at half-time, things soon went rapidly downhill. We found our attention diverted by the splendid collection of toby jugs, tankards and water jugs (28 at last count) dotted along the beams. Football days aside, the Snug is a popular locals' pub which has no music, but does have a decent flat-screen TV (much better than those grainy pull-down jobs), which is only turned up for key sporting events, or interesting news items, such as changes in the cannabis laws. There are signs of all stages of the pub's renovations, from the beautifully intact ceiling and beams, and some original stained-glass windows, to the overly simplified and rather dull modern bar. The lino floor has been more carefully refitted, with a wee carpeted area at one side for the ladies. Overall, it's simple with wee flourishes, such as the lovely old drinks trays above the fireplace (the Pony is particularly special), a yard of ale which takes pride of place above the bar, and some well chosen black-and-white photos of old Dundee (look out for the Teeth). The bar staff were friendly; drinks selection is the usual McEwan's 70/- and 80/-, Guinness, etc., but it's a decent pint, and on weekdays when we were there it was only £1.60. There's also a small but satisfying offering of malts. And if you're lucky, you can hear the roar from Tannadice . . . well, that depends on who's doing the roaring.

Lochee

We weren't going to go out as far as Lochee in our pub travels, but we felt it deserved a mention. Lochee has a number of pubs – some very old, such as the Corner Bar and the Railway Tavern – but few retain much, if any, of their original features. There's also the utterly bizarre Planet bar, which does indeed look like it's from another planet, and the new 'old' pub, Ellen Shannon's on the High Street, which tries to recreate what all these pubs were probably once like. To choose one to visit was tricky, as we heard various stories about the rather lively nature of some of them. The Sporting Lounge sounded the most harmless, and the photographs sounded interesting. So – decision made.

SPORTING LOUNGE
96 High Street
Lochee
Tel: 01382 611412

Owned and run by ex-boxer Frank Hendry, this is one of the quieter Lochee pubs, in terms of friskiness, although the jukebox tends to blare out quite forcefully. The walls are covered with great old boxing photographs and other sporty memorabilia, such as a signed photo of a very young Stephen Hendry sporting a rather alarming jumper. The clientele are a mixture of single, coupled and groups of happily drunk people. Bouts of impromptu dancing are a regular occurrence. The Sporting Lounge is popular for karaoke nights at weekends. There's an unsurprising selection of beer, but we were happy enough with their McEwan's 80/-.

As you stand outside the Sporting Lounge, you will see the signage for the function suite upstairs, the Olympic Suite, where a couple of ice cream cones are doing a passable impersonation of Olympic torches.

Broughty Ferry

EAGLE INN
155 King Street
Tel: 01382 779819

The oldest pub in Broughty Ferry, dating back to the 1600s, The Eagle was probably once a great pub. It's a classic old building with very low ceilings that looks as though it had a makeover in the mid-1990s; plain orange walls, blue carpet in the lounge area and a cocktail menu are all telling signs. It's very much a locals' pub, with an easygoing community feel about the place. It's quite lively, with very loud karaoke on a weekend, and a couple of TVs. It feels a little like being below deck, but not in such a well-preserved ship as the *Royal Arch*.

FERRY INN
27 Gray Street
Tel: 01382 776941

Another great wee Ferry pub, and a member of the low-ceiling brigade, this is Jeff Stewart, the owner, at his best. This small, friendly watering-hole has a cosy atmosphere, with happy and helpful staff who sport Royal Stewart tartan waistcoats (also modelled round the corner in the Ship Inn). The place has a wide range of clientele; when we visited, there were golfers looking to rest their clubs, two old chums with their pub dogs at their feet, and a couple tucking into some of the fine food that's on offer. This is a step up from pub grub, and into the bargain, a new Italian chef has recently been installed in the restaurant upstairs. This was not yet open at the time of writing, but expectations are high. The bar has a living-room vibe with some interesting curiosities on the walls, including a framed telegram sent from snooker ace Ray Reardon to Jeff 'Blackball' Stewart, congratulating him on winning a competition at the Three Barrels (when the pub was in Jeff's hands). There are lots of regulars, and the beer is excellent, with a good choice of ales and spirits, including some fine malts.

FISHERMAN'S TAVERN
10–14 Fort Street
Tel: 01382 775941

The Fisherman's Tavern, or 'the Fish' as it's affectionately known, is such an institution – such a *legend* of a pub, that to do it justice in writing is a nigh-on impossible task. Not only is it a gorgeous, character-laden gem of a building, it also serves some of the finest beer you will drink anywhere in Scotland, let alone Dundee.

A converted fisherman's cottage, its old, wooden, swingy, squeaky doors lead you into the main (and original) bar, which has to have the lowest of the low ceilings so characteristic of the Ferry pubs. There are only a couple of tables in this part of the bar, one which is possibly the smallest table I've ever seen, and an oddly shaped corner one which has recently had its domino-weary surface replaced with a map of the River Tay. Other seating consists of a wee padded bench without a table, and seating round the bar. It's all lino floors and a mish-mash of lovely old wood and some knocked-together panels. Although it has the feel of being a well-preserved old bar, it's not precious. There's no particular style; the effect is best described as endearingly shambolic. The lighting in here is just bright enough to read your book when you've popped in for a peaceful teatime pint.

Over the years, the Fish has gradually expanded. What used to be a small snug to the left, is now a larger, modernised lounge, more suited to those in need of a 'proper' seat. Another addition is to the rear of the original bar – more seating, and a real coal fire. It's the perfect place to sit on a crisp Sunday afternoon after your riverside walk from Dundee. There is also now a hotel attached, with some en-suite rooms, and excellent traditional breakfasts.

The Fish is rightly famous for its outstanding quality and range of real ales. Some are permanent residents, such as Maclay's 80/- and Boddingtons Bitter but the guest ales are always superb, and there are usually at least eight to choose from. To assist you in this, there's a blackboard by the bar which lists all the guest ales, their strength, their price and their regional home. Previous guests have included Marston's Pedigree, Fullers London Pride, Deuchars IPA, Dent Aviator and Bishop's Finger. This small list cannot do justice to the astonishing number of fine ales that have passed through these pumps.

Although now in the safe hands of the reputable Jonathan Stewart, it was a Dick Brodie who was responsible for building up the reputation here for good beer. Long before CAMRA existed, he supplied cask-conditioned ale. His reign spanned from 1948 to 1977.

This pub's accolades include Pub of the Year in Scotland 1992 and CAMRA Real Ale Pub in the UK 1993–94 – and it is the only Scottish pub to have appeared in every edition of the *Good Beer Guide*. As if the beer thing isn't enough, the Fisherman's also managed to win themselves the Wine by the Glass Award in 2000 – *and* serve up quality pub food into the bargain. They don't play music here; the pub simply doesn't need it, and the only TV is in the lounge, but it is rarely on. This is one of those rare pubs where regulars just have to walk through the door and their pint is immediately being poured for them. The only negative side to the Fish is that it's not near enough to my house. As I said before, the Fisherman's is legendary, and understandably so. Enough. Go see for yourself.

FORT BAR
58–62 Fort Street
Tel: 01382 779707

The Fort dates back to around 1700, when it formed part of Gray's Brewery, and became a tavern around 1837. It was most recently redeveloped in 1971 and since 1981 it has been under its current ownership. Split into three in an open-plan style into a bar, a lounge and the Fort Steak Bar, it is well known for its food. The portions are sizeable, the prices cheap, and they offer special pensioner rates and children's portions. Don't expect gourmet dishes, but the popularity of the Fort as an eatery is a good sign. The lounge adjoins the dining area, which in turn leads through to the large bar where many of the pub's activities take place. We visited on the evening of a league domino match being played out. The unmistakable sound of shuffling dominoes filled the air as the league set-up was kindly explained to us. We were informed that there are also darts nights, a whole bunch of quiz nights, and karaoke three nights a week. It felt a bit like being in a community centre, but in an endearing way, and with the bonus that it's actually a pub. The Fort is a friendly place where folk know and look out for each other. Selection of beer is average, McEwan's 80/- and 70/-, etc.

JOLLY'S
51 Gray Street
Tel: 01382 477533

The Jolly's situated on the street is the long-standing part of the pub, and is a popular regulars' pub with darts and dominoes on the go. Once upon a time, it was the only pub open on a Sunday afternoon; needless to say, it was very busy. More recently, the premises to the back of the pub have been taken over and turned into a larger, thoroughly modern Jolly's, which has quickly become *the* young persons' pub, with a late teens, early twenties kind of crowd. It's crazy-busy on a weekend when it takes on a club atmosphere, but thoughtfully it has a separate wee bar in the corner for those seeking a quieter moment.

OLD ANCHOR INN
48 Gray Street
Tel: 01382 737889

This is a completely gutted and redesigned version of the Anchor. Once a great old pub full of character, it's now all pseudo Victoriana and bears no resemblance to the original. However, this large pub serves real ale (there are three on offer). It has very friendly staff, and is a proper pub to which you can take your kids, a refreshing change from those family pubs that have an abundance of plastic fittings, kiddie snacks, and as much atmosphere as an airport lounge. Despite our reservations about the makeover, the new Anchor has a pleasant interior and is light and open with nautical-themed décor, which is the norm at this end of town. It should really be called the New Anchor Inn.

POST OFFICE BAR
218 Queen Street
Tel: 01382 736444

I remember this well as a post office, and much preferred it that way; give me stamps, brown parcel paper and postal orders any day of the week. It remains a magnificent old building, but only from the outside. The interior is large and anonymous, with TVs and loud pop music blaring out, whether it's empty or full, although in the world of supermarket pubs, it's more of a Spar. We visited a couple of times, once while waiting for a bus (a fairly brief and unmemorable encounter) and once on a Sunday afternoon, when it was reminiscent of a youth club, with a smattering of young folk kicking around the trivia machines. There were a couple of decidedly out-of-place old boys drinking alone; we desperately wanted to take them by the arm and lead them down to the Ferry Inn or Royal Arch. Having said that, the Post Office is popular with the older generation as a meeting place for morning coffee. At the end of the day, it's just not my kind of pub, and in fairness, it is popular with the more youthful drinker, albeit some just out of short trousers. Lively and loud on a Friday and Saturday night, this is for the Ferry drinker who wants a party pub rather than a classic boozer.

ROYAL ARCH
285 Brook Street
Tel: 01382 779741

From the outside, this looks like a pretty ordinary boozer. Dating back to 1856, the Royal Arch is in fact a gorgeous old pub with a low wooden ceiling which makes you feel as though you're in a ship's cabin. The splendid gantry displays a well-stocked bar, including over 70 malts and whiskies. The gantry, which itself dates back to 1873, was salvaged from the Craigour, which was facing demolition in the 1980s, and has since been stripped back to reveal its natural splendour. Above the bar hang some good old toby jugs. The lounge is more suited to dining, and the busy décor was a touch overwhelming for us. Now owned by Jonathan Stewart, it's no surprise that the ale is excellent, with a fine selection of regulars (including Belhaven Best and Boddingtons), as well as guest beers (Deuchars IPA, Flowers, etc.). The walls are covered with fabulous black-and-white photos of Dundee's two football clubs over the years (dating back to at least 1937). One wall is given over to a display of caricatures of the locals which have obviously been done by a regular. The Royal Arch was a finalist in Bell's Community Pub of the Year in 2001, and has a great atmosphere, with friendly staff and a good blend of drinkers. If this isn't enough for you, they also offer an impressive menu – with seafood a speciality and imaginative vegetarian dishes.

We didn't really know the Royal Arch before, but now that we do, these pub dogs are happy to be seen propping up its bar.

SHIP INN
121 Fisher Street
Tel: 01382 779176

Of all the fine Broughty Ferry pubs, this wins the gold star for location. You're practically right on the stony beach here, with magnificent views across the Tay (particularly good upstairs) and the Lifeboat shed off to one side. Here since the 1800s, the Ship Inn has seen everyone from smugglers to fishermen and performing pub dogs coming through its warm and friendly doors. This is a gorgeous old pub with wood-panelled walls, its watery location influencing the shippy-themed accoutrements, including some ship figureheads. The beer is excellent, with Theakstons Best Bitter and John Smiths among the good selection. There are also a dozen or so malts. The staff are friendly, and the atmosphere is relaxed. Upstairs is the Waterfront restaurant, which not only has the best views in the Ferry, but a great reputation for its Scottish fare. Booking is recommended – we didn't, but on that sunny Sunday afternoon, we were quite happy to retreat downstairs, and with the light streaming in through the windows onto the old wooden bar, drinking in the Ship was happiness itself.

Many years ago, there was a dog called Penny who would come into the Ship Inn and raise money for the Lifeboat. Customers would throw a penny on the floor, and her trick was that she could pick it up in her mouth, and put it in the Lifeboat collection box. We presume she was suitably rewarded for this good charity work with an ashtray or two of McEwan's 80/-.

2

Where to Eat

This section is very much based on my personal experiences of eating out during my research period. As a result, I have to report on duff meals and surly staff, as well as delightful dinners and heart-warming service. This doesn't mean you should avoid the former places; it doesn't even mean they're bad. They just didn't come up to scratch on my official visit. Think of this section more as a friend telling you about their night out. Maybe they didn't have a great time, but you still might be interested to try it for yourself.

There were a surprising number of situations when either I was given the wrong meal, or it just failed to show up. Regarding the latter, this happened once when I was alone and another time when I was in a group of twelve, so no real pattern emerged.

I hope I've been fair, even when my experience has been disappointing, and that you will feel encouraged to try some new culinary pastures.

It has been suggested that there isn't a single decent place to eat in Dundee unless you go to Broughty Ferry or out of town altogether. It has even been described as a culinary desert. This is both unfair and untrue. It is true to say, however, that there is a lack of choice, and although there are few absolutely outstanding restaurants, you can still find some worthy eating places in the city if you bother to look.

At the time of writing, Dundee had no vegetarian restaurants, but veggie options are mentioned within individual reviews.

The restaurants that follow are listed alphabetically, not by type or area.

RESTAURANTS

AGACAN
113 Perth Road
Tel: 01382 644227

Decorated from top to bottom, back to front and inside out with exquisite, highly coloured original artwork. From the doorstep to the table tops and the toilet cisterns, paintings, mosaic work and wooden constructions adorn this unique restaurant. The owner, Zeki, is himself a reputable painter whose work can be seen on the walls along with a changing gallery of other artists' work. It would seem a pity if the food didn't live up to the tremendous standard set by the interior (and exterior) décor. But of course, it does. Although the menu is simpler than the décor, it is in no way overshadowed by it. A set menu, which isn't over-ambitious, concentrates on traditional Turkish fare. The emphasis, understandably, is on meat – lamb in particular. I have it on good authority from several trusted mouths, that the various lamb and chicken kebabs served up at the Agacan are fantastic. I've never heard a bad word about them. Don't be misled by the inclusion on the menu of a 'cheese salad'. The name doesn't do justice to what is in fact a tasty Greek feta salad, and doesn't involve cheese of the orange grated variety. Although limited for vegetarians, the meze was beautifully prepared, and washed down well with a glass of Turkish beer. It's encouraging to see the chef preparing all the food in full view of the customers (and indeed the passing public) at the front of the restaurant. The highlight for us had to be the Turkish coffee, which came with the most delicious Turkish delight ever to have graced this earth. More used to seeing the shocking-pink, rubbery, non-delightful version, we finally got to see the real thing. Studded with pistachios and covered in coconut, one bite of this ambrosia and we thought we'd died and gone to heaven. (We've no sense of direction . . .)

The Agacan is as close as you'll get to Turkey this side of the Mediterranean. Go now. But book first.

ANATOLIA TURKISH RESTAURANT
91 Nethergate
Tel: 01382 204857

Lucky old Dundee. Not one, but *two* very fine Turkish restaurants. Anatolia is the newer of the two and has a more traditional flavour – although most things do compared to the Agacan. Again, there's a set menu, which offers just the right amount of choice. Mostly kebabs and sote, lamb and chicken, etc., with a similar selection of hot and cold mezes. For vegetarians, they also offer a vegetable moussaka, which was delicious, and served with perfect nutty rice. My meze was beautifully presented, topped with a tomato disguised as a rose – very impressive culinary sculpture. There's a lovely sense of ease at the Anatolia, and despite the fact that we were the only people there when we arrived, we didn't feel as if we were in an empty restaurant. Equally, when other diners arrived, the atmosphere remained very intimate and relaxed. Our waiter was absolutely charming: very attentive, but never in an irritating way, and we had some of the best service we've had in Dundee. He took the time to describe all the ingredients of my meze, which included filo parcels, stuffed vine leaves, some very moreish grilled goat's cheese – and, my favourite, the kizartma, a little aubergine number.

Anatolia is tastefully decorated with richly coloured rugs, plates and travel posters (all Turkish of course), with Turkish wines and beer, coffee and delights and subtle traditional music all adding to the authenticity. The only let-downs were the toilets, which looked as though they'd just been forgotten about. (A mere quibble.) Anatolia is a great place to eat, with happy staff and equally happy diners.

ANDRE'S
134a Nethergate
Tel: 01382 224455

At the time of writing, Andre's had been open for a mere six weeks, and when we first visited they were still encountering a few teething problems. Having been much busier than expected (which is a good sign for Dundee diners), they had subsequently run out of certain dishes on the menu. Since these were such early days, we didn't feel we could chastise them for this, so we chose to return another evening, when, they vowed, they would look after us 'big time'. Andre, the owner and chef, is genuinely charming and cuts a fine figure at the front of this tiny restaurant, with his mass of hair piled up inside his chef's hat. One of the things I've always liked about this venue is that you essentially walk past the kitchen on the way through to the restaurant, which is always a good sign that there's nothing to hide. There's a feeling that everyone really wants you to be happy and to enjoy yourself. The set menu has a number of classic French dishes, such as coq au vin and escargots, but it also makes good use of Scottish produce, such as beef and salmon, incorporating them into French-style dishes. It's a bit limited for vegetarians, but that goes with the territory, the French not being the most embracing of this section of society. There are a couple of choices, and you can also have one of the starters made up to a main course, such as the tasty oyster-mushroom ragout in a pastry shell, which, although a little on the small side, came with a very fresh green salad, packed with flavour.

Other diners were tucking into salmon with a couscous crust, Mediterranean vegetable tagliatelli, and mussels – all of which were perfectly pleasing. Fresh desserts included a decent crème brûlée, and a tarte tatin, which involved much plate scraping. There was a good selection of side dishes, including the fine olive-oil mash.

To my knowledge, this is the third restaurant to occupy this curious Swiss cottage site, the previous one being the lovely Anoka. There's always been something a bit awkward about the space, and although it still lacks a little atmosphere, a real effort is being made at Andre's to give it a classic restaurant feel, with proper white linen tablecloths and napkins (a nice touch), set off by the Parisian café music. Andre's reputation is already growing, and with good food at such reasonable prices, it's no surprise. A welcome addition.

ANTONIO'S RISTORANTE ITALIANO
40 Roseangle
Tel: 01382 226990

Slightly off the beaten track, but it's well worth a jaunt down Roseangle. This is an authentic Italian restaurant, run by Antonio and Rose Ferrara. You actually feel like you're in Italy and may find yourself inadvertently reaching into your pocket for your phrase book. Down some steps from the street, you enter what feels like someone's hallway – past the coat-stand and the fridge freezer and into the rough-cast plaster kingdom of Antonio. I've never been to Italy, but my dining partner assured me this was just like many homely Italian restaurants he'd been in, down to the eclectic collection of hotel function-room chairs. The white walls are punctuated with various plastic fruits and a concoction of paintings; our favourite piece was the pair of ceramic laughing bunnies. There's not a huge selection for vegetarians but what we did eat was excellent: wonderfully saucy pasta, and a mushroom stroganoff (which, mysteriously, was listed in the 'Game' section) served with perfectly cooked rice and fresh, simply prepared vegetables. The tiramisu is home-made, and was an absolute treat. We couldn't fault anything about our food, and the service was cheery. The fact that our waitress spoke very little English, and more often replied in  Italian, merely added to the charm of Antonio's. While you're waiting for your meal, which is always freshly prepared, you can enjoy the spectacular views across the river, and watch the trains as they approach from the railway bridge.

Antonio's also has possibly my favourite ladies' loo in Dundee. The walls look like thick, hardened Angel Delight and the wooden ceiling is bordered with blue nylon rope, with a wee ring of the same rope encircling the light fitting. Net curtains too. Fab.

BEIDERBECKE'S
304 Perth Road
Tel: 01382 646281

Beiderbecke's, as the name suggests, is a swingy, jazzy kind of a place, with great music and loads of interesting paraphernalia around the walls – great for a game of I-spy. They've always been known for their large portions, although the way the prices have crept up recently is quite alarming. Most of the main dishes at the time of writing start at around £11, although pastas are slightly cheaper. There's less choice for vegetarians than there used to be, with very little on the main selection. The last time I ate here was before these changes had taken place and the choice was more extensive, although it seemed that there were quite a lot of dishes with the same ingredients, just a slightly different sauce. The food is good and very filling, and all dishes have suitably funky names, with the pizzas all being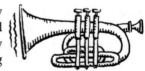

named after singers. Poor old Frank Sinatra is an unfairly plain cheese-and-tomato, while Hoagy Carmichael is at least given the respect of a bit of smoked cheese. Smaller dishes such as Bix's pakora come in at around £3.95 and pizzas range from £5 to £8. There is also a pizza takeaway, with prices lowered accordingly.

Beiderbecke's could be really special, but the inconsistencies in both their erratic opening hours and the recent menu and price changes are a little puzzling. I've had very good and very poor service here, another inconsistency that has hopefully been sorted out. Having said all that, there is an individual feel here that isn't repeated anywhere else in Dundee.

BYZANTIUM
13 Hawkhill
Tel: 01382 228866

Byzantium is surprisingly spacious, given how small it looks from the outside. It's all rough plastered walls and bas-relief stucco with big wooden chairs and tables. There are two types of serving staff: the manically busy young women who don't seem to get a minute's peace, and the slower, patrolling older men who reminded me of the waiters and owners who try to talk you into their Greek restaurant when you're on holiday.

Byzantium describes itself as 'Italian and Modern Mediterranean'. Herein lies the problem. Often one complains about the lack of choice, but here it's just the opposite. Byzantium overstretches itself by offering too long a menu and would benefit from doing fewer dishes really well. Although the food on the whole isn't bad, the quality seemed diluted by trying to cover too many bases. Lobster is on the menu, but has to be ordered two days in advance (all well and good if you don't mind camping out under the billowing canopies for a couple of nights). I ordered an aubergine-based dish, and was understandably surprised at the absence of aubergines . . . perhaps these too needed to be ordered in advance. There are some decent choices on the seafood front, such as swordfish and sea bass, and the mezes were well received (although samosas seemed a little out of place). The pasta dishes, however, lacked sauce and spark. The dessert menu is one of those ubiquitous and ghastly 'Absolutely-not-made-on-the-premises' affairs. Resist. There are obviously some good things going on here (I hear the prawns are very good) but less contenders and more stars could result in something a bit more special.

CAFÉ BUONGIORNO
11 Bank Street
(See 'Cafés' section)

CAFÉ MONTMARTRE
289 Brook Street
Tel: 01382 739313

Arguably the best place to eat in Dundee, this authentic French-Algerian restaurant is in a class of its own. Everything about it is spot on – the food, the service and the ambience. It's quite a classy joint, but in a refreshingly simple and unpretentious way. The food is fantastic, all beautifully presented and wonderfully fresh. Two of our party had couscous dishes – a simple food, but one that's hard to get just right. Both enthused over the perfection of their wheaty grains, the subtle hints of cinnamon, and the thoughtful choice of vegetables and home-made harissa to accompany it. For meat eaters, there's the added choice of chicken, lamb or merguez sausage to go with your couscous. The salmon was succulent, and my baked crêpe, stuffed with well-seasoned spinach, and covered in a perfect béchamel sauce was beautifully balanced. This kind of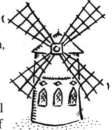

vegetarian dish is often over-cheesy, as though to make up for the lack of meat, but no such measures are necessary here. Likewise, the starters were all splendid, with the French onion soup having just enough of a kick. Others sampled were the mussels, a good-looking goat's cheese salad, and the merguez sausages, which were lean and spicy. Sadly, I had to decline dessert, but found a tiny space for a couple of mouthfuls of a positively dreamy crème brûlée, and the chocolate mousse tasted of real chocolate, without being too heavy. All desserts are obviously freshly made and are thoughtfully presented with sweet little garnishes.

It's not for those on a tight budget, but definitely worth saving up for. Starters and desserts hover around the £5 mark, while main courses start around £9 (which is actually less than some inferior city restaurants) and gradually creep up to the more expensive specials, which can come in at around £19 for the likes of Dover sole. They also do an affordable lunch menu, with lighter dishes on offer.

The décor is simple and warm – there are wooden floors, oil lamps, fresh flowers on the tables, unusually comfortable chairs, and the high ceiling adds to the sense of space and airiness. The front part is decorated with images of Paris, the back with an assortment of black-and-white photos of French celebrities. The atmosphere is relaxed and welcoming and your table is yours for the night, there's none of this rushing you out to make way for a later set of diners.

My general thoughts on eating out are that it should be a treat and a pleasure, and although this is often not the case, eating out at Café Montmartre was a real treat. The fact that it's a bit more expensive than your average Dundee restaurant is totally justified by the fact that it's not your average Dundee restaurant. Due to its popularity, booking is advised. Highly recommended.

CHIANG MAI THAI RESTAURANT
10 Maule Street
Monifieth
Tel: 01382 530500

This is not really within our Dundee boundary, but as there are no Thai restaurants in Dundee, I felt it at least deserved a listing. I've not tried it personally, but this family-run restaurant has a good reputation for its authentic Thai dishes and warm atmosphere.

CIAO SORRENTO
19 Union Street
Tel: 01382 221760

This fabulous wee Italian place somehow lay like undiscovered treasure by us short-sighted ones for years. It was like turning up a trump card that you never knew you had. The surroundings are not typical Italian style; rather it's an eclectic selection of ropy paintings (the sketch of Pavarotti near the window is particularly special), knick-knacks, and some hastily selected music, but it all results in something rather endearing. The menu is excellent, with over 20 pasta dishes to choose from and almost as many pizzas. There is also a wide selection of veal, chicken, seafood (including Dover sole) and meat dishes. The food is good quality, authentic and unpretentious (there are some great saucy pasta dishes). Tiramisu is to be expected on any respectable Italian menu, and Ciao Sorrento's doesn't let the side down. Very moreish. The service was impeccable – unobtrusively attentive, wine glasses filled up by osmosis. If you find yourself out and about and fancy a pizza, skip past the ubiquitous Pizza Hut and turn the corner. Go on . . . go on . . . go on . . .

CUL DE SAC
10 South Tay Street
(See 'Where to Drink' section.)

DANDILLYS
181–183 Perth Road
Tel: 01382 669218

The service in this small bistro is as laid-back as it comes. The night I visited we were served by, I presume, the owner, who seemed to be doing a single-handed job of looking after all the customers (other than the chef of course). As long as you don't mind a pinch of inoffensive cheek and a touch of absent-mindedness, you'll get along just fine. All harmless fun. A good mix of people come here and there are obviously a lot of regulars, which is a good sign. The menu is unchanging, but there's a fair choice of pizza, pasta, seafood, chicken and crêpe dishes. I felt it was perhaps a touch over-priced but the food was pleasant enough, although not remarkable. They serve up decent portions, but not those crazy man-sized ones. The house wine is dire, but fortunately you can bring your own (corkage fee charged), and there's a small selection of bottled beers. The interior is mainly cream; a bit like a big block of vanilla ice cream, with a lot of painted wood (that'll be the wafers). There are nice lamps, and black-and-white photos on the walls. We visited in winter and it was a bit chilly, but that might just be the ice cream effect.

FINE PALATE
204 Perth Road
Tel: 01382 225650

Looking like your typical Chinese from the outside, nothing prepares you for the unlikely interior of this restaurant, which has to be the least Oriental I've ever come across. More reminiscent of a country kitchen café in style, with floral drapes and calor-gas heaters. Behind this quirky setting there's something pretty good going on in the kitchen, resulting in some great Chinese food being served up. The quality is consistently good, and the  unassuming air only adds to the enjoyment. A varied menu includes a decent vegetarian selection – their fried tofu with green peppers in black-bean sauce is up there with the best. There's an extensive menu with all your Chinese culinary favourites. A friend of mine swears by their deep-fried crispy beef. Chinese beer is available and comes in a can which informs you that your beer is made with spring water, which is nice. Dessert choices include delicious flaming-hot deep-fried banana balls (I advise you *not* to put these into your mouth whole – my friend tried this once, and his head almost exploded). A journey to the ladies is always an adventure, as you have to disappear behind some heavy curtains, which lead the way through to a hidden function room. You almost expect to find a scene from a James Bond film being played out. The Fine Palate have a couple of round tables with spinny things in the centre for that communal eating experience (possibly doubling up as a roulette wheel after dark). Given that it's the food that matters most in any eating establishment, the Fine Palate gets a big thumbs-up from me. A good carry-out menu is also available.

GULLISTAN HOUSE
Queen Street Hall
Broughty Ferry
Tel: 01382 738844

A converted church hall (I'm sure I've done some bad dancing here in a previous life), Gullistan started out life in Gray Street, just down from the level crossing, premises which are now the Wee Guli, the younger brother of this far bigger venture. The Queen Street restaurant itself is very traditionally Indian, with the ubiquitous water feature. But all that splashing just makes you want to go to the loo all the time. There's also a large fish tank – with fish to look at but not to be selected for your main course. The main man, who I presume to be the manager, is a real character who always makes you feel welcome. Staff are smart and polite and the service is good. You can always rely on the traditional Indian food here to be up to scratch and the family buffets are very popular. A take-away service is available, with an unusually pleasant waiting area, and food is the same high quality of the restaurant. It does get busy on a weekend, so if you can't get a table, you could always try the little brother round the corner, which I presume is of the same standards.

HET THEATRECAFÉ
Dundee Rep
Tay Square
Tel: 01382 206699

Right in the centre of what is fast becoming the dining heart of Dundee, het theatrecafé has been here for longer than most and is keeping well on top of the competition. One of the best places to eat in town, whether you're in for a lunchtime snack or a full-blown three-courser, the standards here are consistently high. Although housed within Dundee Rep, it is in no way overshadowed by it, and exists happily in its own right. The service is always great and genuinely friendly, and the staff will do their best to meet any specific requirements. Head chef Stef Murray has a creative touch which can transform the simple into the unusual. The soups are always vegetarian and although they sometimes sound a bit peculiar, I guarantee they are some of the finest soups you'll taste in town. The set menu changes monthly and daily specials are always available. Expect anything from home-made fishcakes or grilled salmon with a cider-and-mussel sauce, to vegetable satay or Vietnamese-style beef. If you prefer something simpler, there is always a good choice of salads, sandwiches and pizzas. They even have the cheek to serve some of the best coffee in town and know how to make a proper cappuccino.

The setting has a subtle theatricality – there are thankfully no swathes of cloth or tragedy/comedy masks, but large black-and-white prints of past shows, and a series of terracotta Greek theatre-style masks. Small lighting rigs with theatre lamps hang from the stepped ceiling, which follows the contours of the auditorium above. With breeze-block walls and a varnished wooden floor, the overall effect is refreshingly simple.

Het theatrecafé is popular with a wide range of customers, from groups of business and university folk at lunchtime to large parties out to celebrate anything from a 21st to an 80th birthday. Naturally it's busy with the pre-theatre crowd too. On Saturdays, it's popular with families – it must make a nice change from the usual child-friendly eating places which usually lack good food or atmosphere. In the upstairs foyer, there is another bar, where you can enjoy simpler fare, such as soup and sandwiches. On Friday nights, there is a Jazz Club (more on this in the 'Live Music' section).

If I had my way, I'd move het theatrecafé out of the theatre, and give it an even wider audience.

HOWIE'S
25 South Tay Street

At time of writing, Howie's has a site, but there are no signs of life as yet. Due to open some time in 2002, this branch of the reputable Edinburgh chain will be a welcome addition to the city.

JAHANGIR
1 Session Street
Tel: 01382 202022

The Jahangir has a superb reputation, one I've always felt was well deserved. Having not been there for a couple of years, I chose to combine my official visit with my birthday as a special treat. Unfortunately it didn't go to plan. The service has always been impeccable, but on this occasion our waiter was surly, verging on rude. The food was uninspiring; a vegetable bhuna consisted of a sorry crop of frozen veg (cauliflower and carrots), although the pashwari naan was delightful. It saddens my heart to have to report this, as I'd rather ignore this experience and wave it through with flying colours, based on happier meals.

I've always adored the Jahangir and love its setting – an old industrial shed with a façade like a pink Indian palace. As you enter the restaurant, the experience is akin to disappearing through the wardrobe in the Narnia stories; you not only enter another country, you're in another world. Having been met by the suitably turbaned Dundonian Indian prince at the door, you're unusually seated in a waiting area, where you choose your meal before being taken to your table. This may be to allow customers to admire the celebrity photo (Richard Wilson and our Dundee prince) and the many awards which adorn the walls. The restaurant itself is set around a large fishpond, and embroidered Indian tents are draped across the ceiling. Depending on where you're seated, the lighting is so subtle that you may find yourself fumbling for your chapattis.

The early evening set price buffet is always popular, and nine times out of ten you'll get a cracking meal here. We were probably just unlucky; perhaps being a Sunday night, they were breaking in a new chef, but we would expect a venerable establishment like this, with its many accolades, to be delivering the goods every time.

JUTE
DCA
Nethergate
(See 'Cafés' section.)

LEONARDO & CO.
107 Nethergate
Tel: 01382 201500

With the imminent arrival of DCA, Leonardo's was quick to jump at the chance of opening a branch in the city. It's in a brilliant situation, being a stone's throw from both Dundee Rep and DCA. It also sits between the city centre and the university area, so it would have to try hard to fail. Sadly for them, it has. At the time of writing, the future of Leonardo's is uncertain, but as it remains open in the meantime, a review it shall have.

With its wooden floor, private booths and elegant surroundings, Leonardo's marries modernist simplicity with a more traditional warmth. The main thing that gives it away as a chain is the menu, which seems to have dumbed down since it first opened. Peculiar characters appear on it, telling you not to forget their great special offers – one of which is a 'Last Supper', which I thought sounded a bit ominous. Not one to offer your ailing granny. The menu is made up of an eclectic combination of Scottish and Italian-style dishes, with Highland haggis and clapshot, and smoked salmon, for example, sitting alongside pizza and pasta dishes. Having eaten in Leonardo's a couple of times in the evening, I thought I'd give them a whirl at lunchtime. Smaller dishes include a variety of salads, starters and expensive sandwiches. Despite being quiet, the kitchen managed to completely cock up my order. Actually, it just didn't arrive. After some prompting, it finally materialised, with apologies from the very polite waitress, who insisted I didn't have to pay for my meal. Sadly it wasn't worth the 35-minute wait, and certainly wasn't worth the £4.95 I should have paid. The service is usually fine, but the food is best described as consistently average. It's not terrible, but it's not great – remarkably unremarkable.

MANDARIN GARDEN
40–44 South Tay Street
DD1 1PF
Tel: 01382 227733

This is an excellent Chinese restaurant, serving some of the best food in Dundee's city centre. The seafood is particularly good and if you've ordered something 'sizzling', you'll hear it before you see it. For vegetarians, the bean curd dishes are great, with an abundance of big chunks served up with one of their delicious sauces. One night, four of us went, and everyone wanted bean curd, but they were all out of the stuff. Disaster. The manager, however, proved himself worthy, and produced a magnificent vegetarian banquet for the four of us which is the kind of service you can expect in this fine establishment. I once had the banana fritter for dessert and, for some reason, I was expecting a number of small pieces, but instead was presented with what looked like a sacrificial deep-fried phallus lying in a pool of maple syrup. This was a touch alarming, but once I plucked up the courage to attack the thing, it proved to be very pleasant – the banana firm, the maple syrup adding just enough sweetness.

The décor in Mandarin Garden is understated, with a few Chinese prints of pandas and calligraphic gestures dotted around. A peculiar range of music is played – expect anything from

Richard Clayderman to The Pretenders, or even Aretha Franklin. An extensive wine list adds to the pleasure of dining here, although the staff will advise you against the Chinese liqueurs, due to their strength. They're actually quite palatable, although you may be talking gibberish fairly shortly afterwards.

PIZZA EXPRESS
31 Albert Square
01382 226677

Despite the ubiquity of Pizza Express, as a chain they succeed in giving each of their restaurants an individual touch and manage to avoid the banality of the usual trademark look. Their restaurant in Dundee won an architects' award for best-designed building. It has a bright, sleek, modern interior, with a grand piano of all things, which does sometimes get played. Food standards do vary between branches but the food is good here – not exceptional, but fairly trustworthy, and the pizza toppings are pretty generous. The service is good and reliable. Tucked away near the McManus Galleries, it isn't the most obvious location and as a result can be fairly quiet. This is a pity, as the inferior Pizza Hut is in the middle of the city centre and continues to draw undeserving numbers of customers through its doors.

PIZZA HUT
2 Nethergate
Tel: 01382 200220

Pizza Huts really are the same wherever you go, and this one is no exception. There are far better places to eat pizza in Dundee, but should you wish to part with your money here, it's next to Going Places, the travel agency. You could always pop in and book a holiday to Italy, should you wish to experience the real thing.

RAFFLES
18 Perth Road
(See 'Where to Drink' section.)

ROYAL OAK
167 Brook Street
Tel: 01382 229440

Is it a pub? Is it a restaurant? Well, there's no way I'd describe the food here as 'pub grub', so for the purposes of this guide, it's going to be a restaurant. There is a small section to the left as you enter that's just for drinking, but it's mostly set out with big wooden tables and chairs. The general feel is that of an old country house, what with the stuffed fish in glass cases, an extraordinarily long fishing rod, and an old brass bed-heating pan among the décor. It's a highly unusual setting for Indian cuisine, but the result is wonderfully quirky – and no flock wallpaper required. The atmosphere is informal and relaxed, with the odd person popping in for a pint, while we sat next to the real coal fire (an absolute treat) and tucked into some very fine food. The menu isn't over-ambitious; a good selection of Indian dishes is the main emphasis, although there is only one vegetarian option. This can be made to your preferred strength, and the vegetables were good and fresh – big chunks of aubergine, courgette and pepper soaking up the tasty sauce. All curry dishes are served with pilau rice, chapattis, and a selection of Indian condiments, and are very reasonably priced. Other dishes available include steak pie, haddock, a selection of hot and cold tapas, and steaks. Starters include mulligatawny soup and garlic mushrooms, and there is a standard selection of sweets. The Royal Oak is a warm and friendly place, with a deserved reputation for its food, and it also has a long tradition of serving excellent ale. Caledonian 80/- and Burton's are

regulars, with guest ones always on offer. We sampled Burton's and London Pride, and both went down very well, and proved to be fine accompaniments to curried food. There is a more intimate eating area at the back, which does feel more like a restaurant, but I quite like the homeliness of the bar. Friendly staff and excellent value for money make this a place worth going back to.

TAPAS BAR
16 Commercial Street
Tel: 01382 200527
See 'Where to Drink' section.

CAFÉS, COFFEE SHOPS, TEA-ROOMS

The Coffee Shop Phenomenon

All over the world, but more startlingly in Dundee, there has been a kind of escalating coffee madness. People just can't get enough of the stuff, particularly 'posh' concoctions, such as the now-ubiquitous latte and cappuccino. This goes some way to explaining the monumental rise and rise of coffee chains sprouting all over the city centre. Costas was the first to claim territory in Dundee, opening its frothy doors to the unsuspecting public in Reform Street in 1998. This was a welcome sight, as up until this point the best you could do in the city centre was BHS, Debenhams or Arnotts, and a handful of greasy-spoons. Not an awe-inspiring choice. Since this first branch opened, they've been breeding like proverbial rabbits – there are now three Costa coffee shops within a few hundred yards of each other (Reform Street, Overgate Centre and Waterstone's bookshop) and two branches of Starbucks have recently joined this alarming coffee phenomenon. It's great to be so well served, but it's sad that they're all massive conglomerates, squeezing your last couple of quid out of you for a cuppa, and with barely an independent in sight. The best of these in the centre of town is Café Buongiorno (Bank Street) which, although tucked away from the main bustle, is literally a stone's throw from the coffee superpowers lining up in Reform Street. It serves by far the best coffee in the town centre. The likes of Costa do get a big tick from me, however, for being able to produce, consistently, a decent cappuccino. This should traditionally be made with espresso topped with steamed frothy milk; there is a knack to this. Everyone is so desperate to meet the public demand for 'posh' coffee, that the words 'cappuccino' and 'latte' crop up in the most unlikely places. Beware. These will often be inferior offerings, with your froth draped limply across the surface, only to dissolve like dishwater before your very eyes. Just order a cup of tea instead.

There are, of course, other places to take tea. Just a little further up the road from the parade of giants, you can choose serenity in the form of the Tibetan Tea-room, part of an alternative health set-up. They offer you a variety of very fine coffees from Braithwaites (see p155) in cafétières. Being a Tibetan tea-room, we were expecting to be spoilt with lovely home-made delights of healthiness, but were offered Tunnock's caramel wafers and Kit Kats instead – now, I'm a fan of Tunnock's, but somehow I can't visualise the Dalai Lama tucking into one of their teacakes. Still, this was a peaceful departure from the consumer zen of McDonald's down the street.

BRAMBLES
175 Brook Street
Broughty Ferry
Tel: 01382 730811

This is the king of cafés. It truly is everything you could want in the world of tea and scones and home-made soup. This lovely family-run coffee shop offers an incredibly broad menu, and almost everything is home-made, from the soup (which is always delicious) to the scones, cakes and various pastry dishes. Blackboards around the walls inform you that your drinks can be made with any number of milk types, including soya, and they don't let a diet get in the way of your cake intake, offering fat-free options.

Although you may at first think the prices a little high, the portions are generous, and the food is always extremely fresh and of top quality. They offer an interesting selection of salads, including nut roast and roll mop herring; a number of pasta dishes, pizzas, their own pastry turnovers, and changing daily specials – for example smoked haddock, leek and Gruyère tart, or Thai green curry. Desserts include clootie dumpling, rhubarb crumble, and the special when I was last in was Bailey's Irish Cream meringue roulade. It looked amazing, and tasted even better. The owners, Pete and Carole, both do an incredible amount of home baking; Pete runs the scone department; Carole the cakes and slices. The scones are worth the bus fare to the Ferry, and the pecan caramel shortie I had (and shouldn't have) required a walk home afterwards. If this hasn't tempted you yet, they are also licensed, and serve the superb local Cairn o' Mohr wine, as well as bottled beer and spirits. Children are well catered for, with not only a children's menu (including banana on toast) but also a book corner, which is great if you don't want to have to share your pudding. Brambles is always busy, especially at lunchtime, so be prepared to queue. Staff are bright and helpful and seem to genuinely enjoy their work. Big, colourful paintings adorn the walls, which won't be everyone's cup of tea, but they are preferable to the usual prints-of-Dundee fare.

CAFÉ BUONGIORNO
11 Bank Street
Tel : 01382 221179

Tucked away from the crowds, but well worth seeking out. Café Buongiorno operates as a café by day and miraculously unmasks itself as a restaurant at night (actually, there's not much change after the crossover, other than an extra menu). Serving the best coffee in the town centre, they offer cappuccino and espresso – no need for lattes or mochachocaccinos here – and they come with an Italian biscuit. Scones are served with butter and jam in their own dishes, which is a nice change from the usual pre-packed portions. Other than muffins and scones, the only snack items are the filled ciabattas and paninis, with inventive fillings such as Bel Paese cheese with pistachio nuts, or roast lamb with mint sauce. Pasta dishes include four types of lasagne, and among the pizza choices is an excellent mixed seafood and one of the best fiorentinas (spinach and ricotta) I've tasted. The toppings are both fresh and ample. 'Miscellaneous' meals include aubergine parmigiana, and there are always two specials boards – one for seafood; the other for a range of vegetarian and meat choices. Home-made tiramisu and amaretto ice-cream lead the desserts board. There's Italian beer and a wine list on request.

The overall feel of Café Buongiorno is that of an outdoor pavement café, with its stone-tiled floor, round faux-marble tables and terrace-style chairs. This is not the Mediterranean, however, so if you can't put the café on the pavement, bring the pavement café inside. Amongst the staff, there didn't seem to be an Italian in sight, but the service is always polite and friendly and the music is an endearingly eclectic mix of Italian warblings, and Scots-Italian accordion sounds.

CORNERSTONE COFFEE HOUSE
118 Nethergate
Tel: 01382 202121

Run by the church next door, this coffee shop is a popular spot with the older brigade, who meet up regularly here for tea and scones and a good old natter. It's very utilitarian, but has big paper lampshades and flowers on the tables to soften the edges. Upstairs is the smoking area, but there's a spiral staircase that leads you downstairs to the main, smoke-free zone. There's also a side entrance opposite the underpass. They serve good, honest fare – toasties, omelettes, baked tatties, and their soup comes with delicious Dr Floyd's bread (see under Fisher & Donaldson for more on this delight). Coffee is filter only, which is actually quite a refreshing sight these days. The Cornerstone is wholly unpretentious and efficiently run by an army of volunteers who I suspect even bring in the home baking.

COSTA
Reform Street (between McDonald's and the Skipton Building Society)

This is the first of three Costas in town and is the only one that serves more substantial meals, such as pizza and pasta. The others are at:
   The Overgate Shopping Centre
   @ Waterstone's Booksellers, 35 Commercial Street

The Waterstone's Costa is the most pleasant of the three, away from the throng of other people's shopping bags. The mezzanine setting and ambience of the bookshop add to the more relaxed nature here. There are good comfy chairs too, and newspapers to read.

FISHER & DONALDSON
12 Whitehall Street

Attached to the very fine bakers, the café area here is quite small, but they've managed to squeeze in quite a few tables. This place is very popular on account of the quality cakes you can treat yourself to while enjoying a cup of their good coffee or tea. Tasty filled rolls made with the excellent Dr Floyd's seven-grain rolls are served up by friendly, chatty staff. The shop on the Perth Road also has a small café tucked away at the back.

GOODFELLOW AND STEVEN (CAFÉ VIENNA)
83 Gray Street
Broughty Ferry

As with Fisher & Donaldson, the café here is attached to the shop, although this one's more spacious. Again, fine coffee and tea helps wash down those special treats from the bakers.

HET THEATRECAFÉ
Dundee Rep
Tay Square
(See 'Restaurants' section.)

JUTE
DCA
152 Nethergate
Tel: 01382 432281

DCA/Jute is a bar, café and restaurant. We decided it was more of a high-class café than a restaurant, thus its entry in this section. Given the critical acclaim of DCA as a building, and as it's seen by many as one of the best things to have happened to the city for a long time, Jute should really be great, but sadly it isn't. I like the space – it's bright and airy and has an open, modern, industrial warehouse look. It also has the advantage of having one of the most stunning views across the river. It's a great place to sit of an afternoon, whether you're with friends or alone with a coffee and a good book. Where it falls down is service. It was notoriously bad when DCA first opened, but unfortunately this has gone beyond teething problems – they should have their wisdom teeth by now. The service is most fairly described as inconsistent. I've had some great service here from attentive, friendly staff, but at other times it was verging on appalling. A friend and I once spent 25 minutes, on a very quiet afternoon, waiting for a cup of tea. When we reminded the staff of our presence, they eventually brought the tea, only it was the wrong kind. The waiting time for evening meals can be frustratingly long, especially if you've ordered from the pre-theatre menu, and you can end up missing the start of the play and spend the rest of it picking spinach out of your teeth. You'd think with the number of complaints they must've had since opening, they'd have sorted themselves out by now.

This may all sound harsh, but the food can be very good – although some of the main meals are a little over-priced for the small portions. They also suffer from an increasingly common syndrome, 'over-elaborate descriptions of the food'. I once ordered 'roasted vegetable skewers on a bed of winter leaves'. Aye, right. How about ' vegetable kebabs with salad'? It was very tasty, but spare me the poncification please.

I've heard many reports and experiences of eating in Jute, and they're all different so I suggest you try it for yourself. Some decent snacks can be had at any time of the day, the potato wedges being a particular favourite. Cheap and cheerful, unlike the bar prices.

As a bar, DCA is dearer than most proper pubs. On Friday and Saturday nights, the bar is transformed into *the* pre-club, boy-and-girl-about-town place to be seen and it is always heaving. The cinemas in DCA are right next to the bar, and it can be a bit of a shock to the system if you've been watching a film of a more melancholic nature (*Life is Beautiful; Iris*), to be suddenly thrown mercilessly into this party arena. A hasty retreat to the Phoenix is usually the answer. DCA is a decent place to drink on a week night, and on a lazy Sunday afternoon you can enjoy live music while sipping a glass or two of red. In the summer, the doors are opened onto the concrete patio, where you may even be treated to a live DJ.

JUTE @ McMANUS
McManus Galleries
Albert Square

When I first visited this café, it was called Café on the Square. Although it all looks much the same, the menu has changed entirely, now being of the hip-and-trendy panini-and-wrap variety. Some of this was creeping in before, but what they did best was the more simple fare – baked tatties, toasties, the humble filled roll and some reasonable cakes. When I returned to it in its current guise of Jute, I ordered the carrot-and-coriander soup, which tasted okay, but was decidedly lukewarm. This probably wasn't helped by the bowl, which was so wide and shallow, that it probably cooled down between kitchen and table. The menu is fairly minimal, with three paninis and pasta dishes, and five sandwich fillings to choose from, which can be of the wrap, baguette or granary variety. If you don't like hummus and olives, you're stumped on the vegetarian front. They did a small line of cakey fare when I was there, which all looked bought-in and very sweet – for example *pain au chocolat* with icing. How very Scottish. The staff were mostly young and disinterested – my waitress was trying to get into the *Guinness Book of Records* for cutlery dropping – and without meaning to sound prudish, I'd rather her bare belly hadn't been brushing up against my lunch, thanks.

The modern interior is as it was – thoughtfully designed furnishings that sit well with the majesty of the large arched windows, with good views overlooking the square. There are one or two glass cabinets housing exhibits from the museum/gallery which is a nice touch.

Jute @ McManus is clearly aimed at the younger market, but its location is more suited to traditional fare and home baking. I've never understood why they haven't thought to theme the menu around the contents of the museum. They could be serving up Tay Whale fritters, pastry bridge stumps, Admiral Duncan doughnuts, and mummified meringues. Just a thought.

THE PARLOUR
56 West Port
Tel: 01382 228062

The Parlour is a proper local café. It's small and bright and has a lived-in feel, with simple whitewashed brick walls. It has a complete lack of pretence, as do the staff, who are friendly without fussing; it's a bit like being round at your friend's house when you're a kid and mum pops her head round the door to offer you some cake. The menu is mainly made up of baked tatties (proper ones), toasties and filled rolls, with a few diversions such as fine home-made soup, flans and chilli. The Parlour has many regulars, some of whom are on first-name terms with the staff (all two of them). Their popularity may be down to their very reasonable prices, or possibly the home-made cakes and scones – the coffee-and-walnut was spot-on, the carrot-and-banana was also good, but contained a very large piece of carrot, which I presume must have been meant for the soup. There are daily specials, such as bread-and-butter pudding, to tempt you even further. I admire their refusal to join in with the latest food fashions, such as paninis and sun-dried tomatoes – they stick to what they and their faithful customers like best: good, honest fare, all washed down with some pretty tasty (and freshly made) coffee. This is one of the few cafés where you can get home-made soup and crusty bread, a large slice of cake, and a cafétière of coffee for well under a fiver.

PARROT CAFÉ
91 Perth Road
Tel: 01382 206277

An extremely friendly café, which over the last few years has expanded due to its popularity. Nearly everything here is home-made, from the mayonnaise to their excellent soups. There are usually two soups to choose from, they come highly recommended – and, if requested, with excellent home-made bread. They also do flans, baked tatties, and an assortment of sandwiches, including some on delicious rye bread. If you can, you should always leave a wee space for some of their very tasty home baking. Scones, cakes, fruit breads and a moreish gingerbread are all regulars and there are daily specials thrown in for good measure. Depending on what you order, you won't always get as much as you would like, for example the toasties are open and constitute only one slice of bread, in which case you will definitely require cake consumption. It's best to ask just what your dish will consist of. It's very reasonably priced (with, at the time of writing, soup coming in at £1.30 and scones at 75p – an absolute bargain). If you don't take kindly to folk puffing away while you tuck into your sandwich, this is the place for you, as there is a no-smoking policy throughout. (I once knew someone who said that they didn't like people eating while they were smoking – what's that all about?) The Parrot has a great atmosphere, loads of regulars, and cheery banter from all the staff, ensuring a most agreeable time.

RUSSELL'S
242 Perth Road
Tel: 01382 644886

Russell's is a Perth Road institution, a traditional family-run café serving all your favourite tea-room treats. It's a bright and sunny room with no fancy décor, which is exactly what you want when eating home-made cake. There's a huge board on one wall with definitions of different coffees (latte, espresso, etc.) which is writ so large, you can probably read it whilst supping a pint in the Taybridge Bar across the road. They do, however, make a good cappuccino. Standards here are baked tatties, which we felt were a bit over-priced; various sandwiches, and some more substantial dishes, including Thai fish cakes, and vegetable lasagne. The daily specials board displays the home-made soup and pudding highlights of the day.

We tried the apple crumble and custard, which unfortunately had lost its crunch in the microwave. Sunday breakfast was fine, if a bit average. I do recommend the hearty soups, and excellent home-made cakes and scones. I had one of the best scones I've had in years here, and they also do a mean fruit loaf. Just like your granny used to make.

Russell's has lots of devoted regulars, which makes for an all-round happy eating experience. It does tend to get busy of a lunchtime, so perhaps the best time to dip your toe into Russell's waters is for afternoon tea.

STARBUCKS
Overgate Shopping Centre
Wellgate Centre

The Overgate Starbucks is notable for having a handful of comfy armchairs which face out onto the City churches, which is really quite pleasant on a sunny afternoon. They also have seating outside if you fancy fresh air, or a smoke.

TOP OF THE TOWER CAFÉ
Tower Building
Dundee University
Perth Road
Tel: 01382 344166

I suppose it was once regarded as a tower, but these days it's decidedly low-rise. The café is situated on the tenth floor, which is as high as this tower goes. Part of the university, the Tower Café is mainly used by staff and students of both here and the Art College, although it is also open to the general public. It's worth coming here for the views alone, especially if it's a clear, bright day and you are seated along the breakfast bar area round the windows. The main café area has spectacular views overlooking the river and to both bridges to the south and west. In the north-facing room, you look both west and east – maybe not as stunning as in the south-facing space, but still far preferable to merely looking at four walls.

The whole place was redesigned a few years back by a group of Interior Design students from Duncan of Jordanstone College of Art, and it is clean and bright; reminiscent of an upmarket and stylish classroom, with its simple, square tables and designer school chairs with primary-red seats. The food here has a great reputation, not just because it's so cheap, but also because it's pretty good quality too. When you sit down, you'll find a list of the day's offerings. You mark off your choices, and hand it over. When I visited, the main dishes included lamb chops with redcurrant and coconut sauce, and vegetarian stroganoff, which was served with delicious wild rice. A selection of three-sided snacks are available where you order combinations of smaller dishes, such as soup, chicken kiev and salad. Also on the menu are baked tatties, pasta dishes, and a selection of desserts, such as sticky-toffee pudding. Understandably, the Tower is very popular and busy at lunchtimes. On your way up, or down, be sure to have a look at the Landseer painting on the ground floor, opposite the lifts. It's called *The Trickster*, and is a pub dog if ever I saw one.

TWIN CITY CAFÉ
4 City Square
Tel: 01382 223662

The Twin City Café is loosely based on the rather peculiar practice of cities being twinned with each other. Dundee has somehow managed to twin itself with Zadar in Croatia, Wurzburg in Germany, Orleans in France, Nablus in the Middle East, and Alexandria in the USA. The mind boggles as to what we have in common with them. Whatever the reasons though, the menu of the Twin City Café has been themed accordingly. Many Middle Eastern offerings, such as stuffed vine leaves and falafel are interspersed with the more familiar cheese rolls and filled tatties (not the cheapest in town).

The multi-cultural thing has been half-heartedly adopted into the décor, with a time-zone display of clocks representing each city and its relative time – on my visit, all set incorrectly, including Dundee. There's also an odd still-life arrangement with some carved camels jostling for attention with some brass jugs and an ornamental hookah. An assortment of framed pictures, with a predominant theme of camels and pyramids, attempt to heighten the cosmopolitan flavour of these Dundonian walls.

The Twin City is fairly busy, mainly due to its central location in the City Square rather than its offerings. It's popular with groups of elderly women and office workers. Despite the table service, it feels a little like an upmarket staff canteen; the tabarded girls behind the counter made me think of *Dinnerladies* and I half expected Victoria Wood to pop up at any moment. For some reason, they've worked hard on making their cake cabinet look as unappetising as possible, with the last piece of cheesecake left forlornly next to the plastic milk cartons like the schoolkid no one wants on their team. This all sounds a bit disparaging; it's not actually that bad. It's a touch expensive for what you get, but otherwise acceptable fare.

VISOCCHI'S
40 Gray Street
Broughty Ferry
Tel: 01382 779297

Justifiably famous for its fabulous ice cream – it's worth a visit to the Ferry for this alone – Visocchi's is also a café, serving a decent selection of suitably Italian dishes – large bowls of pasta, great pizzas, ciabattas and the like. All tasty and filling. There's good coffee too, and a small selection of continental breads, chocolate and biscuits in the shop area. There are also tubs of ice cream to take away – can you resist?

WASHINGTON
41 Union Street

Not the place it used to be, but if it's bacon butties and a bit of banter you're after, look no further than the Washington. Long established and well run, this is your classic city café. Individual booths with formica-topped tables and PVC seating set the scene for a thoroughly enjoyable and down-to-earth eating experience. There can't be many places left where you can get a decent cup of tea for around 65p and a freshly filled roll for about a pound. Baked tatties, soup, scones and doughnuts are also available in this popular, no-frills establishment. The cheery staff and its many regulars give the Washington a priceless atmosphere; it's no wonder some of them come here every day. They also sell Tunnock's teacakes (just in case the Dalai Lama drops in).

WILLOWS
146–148 Brook Street
Broughty Ferry
Tel: 01382 732525

This is not in the same league as its closest neighbour, Brambles, but if you can't get a seat there, you could do worse than to pop into Willows for a bite to eat. Part of a small chain, Willows is fairly unremarkable to look at, although it's tidy and bright, and there are some colourful patchwork-type pieces adorning the walls. They have a lengthy list of teas and coffees to choose from and a range of light snacks and more substantial fillers. You can have anything from a poached egg on a roll (you might want to tuck in your napkin in the style of Stan Laurel for this), to a steak-and-mushroom baguette or macaroni cheese. We were disappointed to discover that the tasty-sounding hot mushroom-and-cheese roll was due to be sentenced to the microwave, so we ordered the soup instead, which did the trick. They also do baked potatoes, and a decent range of filled rolls, baguettes and bagels. Most of the cakes looked incredibly sweet, but if this isn't your fancy, you can opt instead for a pancake, scone or toasted teacake. The smoking section is a healthy distance away from the main no-smoking area. The service is fine – polite, but lacking in the personal touch. Not a home-made-fare kind of a place, but a reasonable snack stop.

In-store Cafés

ARNOTTS (HOUSE OF FRASER)
High Street

As I sat down with my pre-packed sandwich, the dulcet tones of the extractor fan distracted me from the screaming child at the next table. The sound was strangely reminiscent of the boiler room of the

Zeebrugge Ferry – it was, however, a refreshing, if somewhat unorthodox, break from the in-season Christmas songs that were disturbing the air elsewhere. My sandwich was perfectly fine, but I also ordered a cappuccino. Cappuccino my arse. The girl merely pressed a button, *et voila* – one distinctly unfrothy, uncoffee-like 'cappuccino'. I know House of Fraser isn't the only place guilty of this, but it really gets my goat – the number of places serving up stuff that is surely in breach of some sort of description act. The closest this cappuccino had got to an espresso was the machines they sell on the third floor.

Having said all this, the staff were friendly and polite and the place was busy. The average age of the customers when we were there was 73. This would have been higher, but there were a couple of young children to redress the balance.

DEBENHAMS/CAFÉ VENUE
Overgate Shopping Centre

Although this is an in-store café, it's actually outside the store. It's not a particularly intimate experience, being stuck in the middle of a busy shopping mall, with a low orange wall serving only to stop old ladies from stealing your teacake. It's a bit exposing, hundreds of passers-by witnessing the development of your cappuccino-froth moustache – but at least they have the decency to sell a proper cappuccino here. They also do a range of sandwiches and nice-looking cakes. A very large umbrella/parasol affair, which serves no particular purpose, occupies the central space. Given a better location, this could be a decent café.

MARKS AND SPENCER/CAFÉ REVIVE
Murraygate

In-store cafés don't greatly inspire me, but as this was a newcomer to the scene at the time of writing, I decided to put them to the cappuccino test. I have to say, it was extremely good. You could seriously taste the coffee through its proper creamy froth. I'd even go as far as to say it's one of the best cappuccinos in the city centre. They also do lattes, espressos, mochas, or simple filter coffees. There wasn't much left of the cakey fare when I visited, but they had some fairly decent-looking sandwiches. You still feel like you're in the middle of a shop, with only a few screens between you and the Harry Potter pyjamas and men's vests. However, the staff are polite and friendly and, as the name suggests, it's a fine place to revive yourself when you're all shopped-out.

Internet Cafés

At the time of writing these hadn't quite caught on in Dundee yet. The only one I could find was in Debenhams (one of three café/restaurants attached to the store). Intercafé is designed to appeal to the younger surfing generation and, in fairness, is not intended to be a relaxing place to stop off for a coffee and a chat. A girl dressed slightly incongruously in an American burger joint kind of get-up was selling Kit Kats, the odd sandwich and some buns, but it's mainly cold drinks and coffee, served in paper cups. I didn't risk the cappuccino challenge here, opting instead for a simple black coffee, which was surprisingly pleasant. At the time of writing, internet access is £1.50 for 30 minutes. Extra charges for printing come in at 25p a sheet for black-and-white, and 50p for colour. Old people like to surf too, so someone really ought to rise to the challenge and provide a service for the rain-mate wearers of the world.

FISH AND CHIPS

The humble chip, that great institution of ours, actually began its British life in Dundee, by way of a Mr de Gernier. This Belgian immigrant came to the city and duly set up a pitch in the Greenmarket, where he sold the first chips, peas and vinegar – giving birth to the 'buster'.

In Dundee, the fish-and-chip shop is known as the 'chipper', as opposed to the 'chippy'. You will be offered salt and vinegar on your chips, or other deep-fried delights, and not salt and sauce. The first time I visited a chipper in Edinburgh, I couldn't understand why they were offering me salt and sauce – how can you eat chips without vinegar? Sauce, for me, just doesn't have the same appeal. We asked our local 'Salty Dog' to investigate the chippers of Dundee on our behalf. There were too many for him to visit without us footing the bill for his private health care afterwards, so left the choice to his discerning palate. We have great pleasure in introducing you to – Salty Dog . . .

DUNDEE CHIPPERS – A PERSONAL ACCOUNT BY SALTY DOG

It must be emphasised at this early stage that the eating of a chipper meal is a very personal thing, and can be affected by many elements, which are often outwith the control of the individual. It is also eminently true that no matter where you travel to, the chippers there will, in one way or another, be inferior to the ones 'round your way'. Especially if you're from Yorkshire, in which case everything will be inferior, particularly the chippers – oh, and the pubs. I must therefore make clear that this review is 90 per cent personal opinion and 10 per cent fact.

Dundee has approximately 29 chip shops. Unfortunately, due to the finite amount of cholesterol the human body can process, it has been physically impossible for me to sample them all. Therefore this review takes into account only a small selection, but it will hopefully give you an overview of the Dundee chipper scene.

THE AMALFI FISH BAR
Arklay Street (up from Dens Road market and across from Tannadice football ground)

This is a cheeky little number – really good food, and a spot of genuinely funny banter from the staff thrown in. I actually found myself laughing, not out of politeness, not because I didn't understand – but because it was funny . . .

Helpful hint: As the Amalfi is directly across the road from Dundee United's football ground, it's best to avoid it on a Saturday afternoon during the football season – unless you're at the game, in which case, it's the perfect time to visit.

FISH OUT OF FIVE:

THE ASHVALE
Arbroath Road (past Safeways, just before the Boar's Rock and the big roundabout)

A relative newcomer on the Dundee chip scene, this award-winning chipper is pretty much the cat's pyjamas. Like any other mortal chipper, it's not infallible and can produce a 'bad un' from time to time, but it is without a doubt the top banana of Dundee chip shops – especially for fish. There are five varieties of fish to choose from: cod, rock turbot, lemon sole, plaice – and, of course, haddock. If you opt for the cod, you're charged by weight. The food is fresh and tasty, the prices are reasonable, and the staff are pretty good. What more can I say?

FISH OUT OF FIVE:

THE BRAE STOP FISH BAR
Hilltown (as the 45-degree monster of a hill starts to ease up, just before the furniture shop).

This is a pretty damn fine chipper in my opinion, well worth checking the weather report, putting on your climbing gear, and tackling one of the steepest climbs known to man, the 'Hilltown'. The staff here are pretty cheery, and there are always plenty of them, so even if there's a queue, you never have to wait that long. The standard of the scran is good, and the portions are big – not so big that you feel like you're trying to beat Elvis's record for calories consumed in one meal, but big enough to make you feel you've got value for money.

FISH OUT OF FIVE: 🐟 🐟 🐟 🐟

THE DEEP SEA
Nethergate (next to the Bank of Scotland, across the road from Groucho's record shop)

One of the oldest chip shops in Dundee, and something of a legend. The Deep Sea is more a restaurant than a take-away, with just a small hatch at the front for paper-wrapped treats. A popular lunch and tea-time stop for sit-down fish and chips, The Deep Sea possibly also has the oldest clientele of all Dundee chippers, although I'm not sure how they can afford it. Despite the Deep Sea's old-school vibe, it has very contemporary prices for the sit-down option. You are, however, given the pleasure of aproned waitress service, bread and butter with your fish and chips, and a proper pot of tea. I recommend one of the wee booths at the back of the restaurant if you choose to sit in. The Deep Sea is a mighty fine chipper, and although the portions ain't the biggest, they are among the tastiest, with the added bonus of having been cooked in vegetable oil. It's well worth a visit. The city's more mature chip patrons give the place a nostalgic and trustworthy feel. The downside to The Deep Sea is its early evening closing; this isn't one for the post-pub chip eater. Very much a lunch/teatime affair.

FISH OUT OF FIVE: 🐟 🐟 🐟 🐟 🐟

THE DISCOVERY FISH AND PIZZA BAR
Nethergate (across from the Overgate shopping centre, City Churches, and taxi rank)

A chip shop of convenience, I feel, due to its liberal opening hours and location. Mind you, it's only convenient if you happen to be out in the centre of town and are trying to get a taxi home after 15 pints. When I was there, the staff seemed suitably miserable, and the food tasted like it had been carefully selected by Del Boy from the cheapest frozen-food supplier in the world. You wouldn't go out of your way to eat here, unless you were determined to end your night out by queuing with 120 drunk and hungry punters.

FISH OUT OF FIVE:

THE PARK FISH AND CHICKEN BAR
Arbroath Road (across from Baxter Park, right on a pedestrian crossing)

This is a really good chipper – the staff are friendly and the food is great. If you prefer sauce to vinegar, you're out of luck here, as they just don't do the sauce thing. The portions are petite, but so are the prices; this is one of the cheapest chippers I've ever been in.

Top tip: If you've been up at Baxter Park watching the fireworks on Guy Fawkes' night, and towards the end you think to yourself, 'Ah'm hungry! Ah feel like a chipper!', then start to make your way towards the gate, because if you dilly-dally and allow yourself to be mesmerised by the final crescendo of pyrotechnic magic, then it'll be game-over, my friend. You will have missed your window of opportunity and the end of the queue for The Park Fish and Chicken Bar will be somewhere near Aberdeen.

FISH OUT OF FIVE:

THE SILVERY TAY
Charleston Drive (over the back of The Law, north-east of Ninewells)

In contradiction to what its name suggests, this chipper is not linked to the silvery Tay; you do not have a panoramic view of the silvery Tay as you order your chips; it is not even particularly near the silvery Tay. In fact, of all the chippers covered in this review, it is the furthest away from the silvery Tay. These points, however, are irrelevant if it's a decent chipper, which it is. The food is good, and the staff are nice, so if you're in the vicinity, and hungry, pay it a visit.

FISH OUT OF FIVE:

THE VICTOR FISH BAR
Blackness Road (up the hill a bit from the fire station, on the other side of the road)

How much you get here depends on who serves you. This makes going in a bit dicey, as you have to be on your toes. You have to weigh up the situation, asking yourself, 'Who's working? How many other people are in? What are their orders?' Hang back, cause a diversion ('you can go before me, madam, I haven't quite decided yet. . . .'), stall, stall again – then strike. Still, all that effort, and it's not always worth it. A pretty decent chipper on the whole, although sometimes a bit hit-and-miss.

FISH OUT OF FIVE:

There are at least another 20 chip shops in Dundee. Will I live to see the day I have eaten at them all? Is it the type of thing I should tell people about? Anyway, before I go, I feel there is one thing I must clarify. Although I am a great lover of chips, and a regular patron and advocate of deep-fried food, do not think for one minute that I'm 25 stone, with congealed lard for arteries, and I have a face and teeth resembling those of Steptoe senior. On the contrary, it has been hours since my last heart attack, and I've had the feeling back in my legs for weeks.

3

What to Do and
Where to Go

ART GALLERIES AND MUSEUMS

McMANUS ART GALLERIES AND MUSEUM
Albert Square
Tel: 01382 432084

This is Dundee's most impressive Victorian structure, with a
stunning sweep of a staircase on its west side. The museum takes
you through Dundee's past, from archaeological displays and Pictish
stones, to the Tay Bridge Disaster. On the ground floor, there is the
impressive but incredibly sad skeleton of the famous Tay Whale
(formerly housed in the now defunct Barrack Street Museum),
which was savagely hunted up and down the Tay and was finally
washed up in 1883. The Tay Whale has been
immortalised by the infamous William McGonagall,
who chose the poor creature's chase and demise as the
subject of one of his dreadful but bizarrely well-known
poems. Alongside the Tay Whale, there are a number
of stuffed birds and mammals, from a water shrew to
a red deer. Not really my sort of thing; it seems odd
that a nature gallery is full of dead stuff – apart from

the frogs and toads, which look like they might be plastic (a bit hard to stuff, I imagine, although I recently discovered that there's a museum in Switzerland which is full of dead, stuffed frogs, dressed in period costume, and arranged in various domestic scenes). Other than this, the ground floor is largely given over to detailing Dundee's history. The loving recreation of a typical old Dundee pub is a must-see, as is the grocer's shop, with a few battered old tin signs (I liked the Palethorpes Royal Cambridge Sausages one). There are small displays covering sport, entertainment and domestic life, with a reconstruction of a tenement kitchen, complete with wally dugs, and cabinets displaying items such as a bundle of nineteenth-century sulphur spunks and a goffering mangle. Wartime memorabilia includes a very dinky chess set, specially made for servicemen. You can also see Mary Slessor's compass, and a cabinet containing a curious assortment of fireworks and some fusty cake. One of the loveliest items is a 1930s–40s hot-water-bottle in the shape of Little Red Riding Hood. There are also some unpleasantries in the form of nameless torture instruments – various head contraptions, and what I suspect may be the biggest padlock in the world. Next door, some wind sound effects start up, to let you know you're in the Archaeology section. There are various relics from digs around Dundee, Angus and Fife – including a spectacular jet necklace, some burial chambers complete with skeletons, and lots of flint and old bits of pots. A wonderful painting by local artist Laura Walker shows a bunch of mischievous-looking Romans unloading their cargo. Unfortunately, you can't stand far enough back to see this properly, but it still looks pretty tasty. Ancient Egypt finds its way to Dundee in the form of a mummy-finding reconstruction and a false tomb door, outside of which people left food for their dear departed. These relatives have been left some plastic fruit. Some Pictish stones and a very long log boat later, and we're ready to go upstairs.

An impressive staircase leads up to the magnificent Albert Hall, with its Gothic Arch roof of pitch pine panels. The hall contains the table at which the death warrants of captured Jacobites were signed after the Battle of Culloden. Further exhibits here include antique musical instruments from around the world, including a nineteenth-century Tibetan trumpet, a North African spike fiddle, and a bronze Burmese gong in an exquisitely carved teak frame. Other curiosities include a selection of knives from the Congo and a couple of unusual paintings by J.A. Wink: *Still Life with Rabbit* (unusual in that the rabbit is actually still alive), and its partner painting involving a squirrel tucking into some nuts. As you make your way along the corridor, you pass some paintings depicting Dundee through the years, including a lovely naïve painting titled *Dundee by the River* (artist unknown). Gallery Six houses the Victorian paintings, some of the finest of these being William McTaggart's wild seascapes. You'll also find Rossetti's *Dante's Dream* and works by Millais and Landseer. The two contemporary galleries show a diverse range of interesting exhibitions, with many touring shows coming here. The year 2002 sees the reputable annual Royal Society of Watercolourists' exhibition visiting the McManus Galleries for the first time in over 50 years, which is a huge boon for the gallery, and for Dundee. There are often guided tours of, and workshops relating to, current exhibitions here. The McManus has a fantastic collection, much of it in storage, but I believe they have work by Stanley Spencer and possibly even a Marc Chagall lurking somewhere in their dusty stores.

Back on the ground floor, there's a decent shop that sells books of local interest, greeting cards and the usual assortment of gallery-related pencils and rulers – and if you go through the corridor that leads to the café, a kind of local 'Past Times' displays replicas of old wooden yo-yos and the like, which you can buy.

DUNDEE CONTEMPORARY ARTS (DCA)
Nethergate
Tel: 01382 606220

Built on the site of a former garage, Richard Murphy's award-winning arts centre has breathed new life into Dundee, as well as encouraging new faces to visit the city. The arrival of Dundee Contemporary Arts in 1999 heralded the beginning of a new cultural identity. Sited as one of the finest exhibitions spaces in the UK, its remit is to show international artists' work which has not previously been seen in Scotland. In my opinion, the most successful exhibitions here have been the one-person shows, rather than the group exhibitions, possibly because most of these have been put together with this specific space in mind. The exhibition of tremendous photographs by W. Eugene Smith is obviously an exception. The images span many years, but it is a hugely successful and moving show nonetheless. More contemporary solo shows have come from Richard Deacon, who filled the floor space with his writhing, twisty wood sculptures; Ian Davenport whose minimal but glorious colourfields of poured gloss paint looked good enough to eat – and more recently, one of Scotland's most highly respected artists, Will MacLean, the only local artist to have been granted an exhibition here, with his very beautiful and thoughtful homages to the sea, including a couple of first-time video pieces.

The exhibition space is split into a smaller and larger gallery, which allows natural light in from above, and has two additional small spaces at the end of the main gallery. These are both glazed from floor to ceiling, giving you a wee glimpse of the city before returning to your viewing. A study room is provided, which has books, videos and newspaper articles relating to the current exhibitions. To the left is a workshop room, which is used both as a community resource room by schools etc., and also by DCA itself for its programme of artist-led workshops. DCA is also the new home for Dundee Printmakers

Workshop, previously attached to the former Seagate Gallery. This is for the use of members and has facilities for all kinds of printmaking – including lithograph, screenprinting and etching – and there are also darkroom facilities. In addition to all this, they run various printmaking workshops, open to the general public. Downstairs is the Visual Research Centre (VRC). Run by the university, it houses two small gallery spaces which show work by artists directly associated with research at Duncan of Jordanstone College of Art. There is also a library resource of books that have been made by artists, which anyone can make use of.

Back on the ground floor, the main entrance level, there is a shop (which is mentioned in more detail in the 'Where to Shop' section). Upstairs from here is yet another small gallery, which specifically shows work by members of the Printmakers Workshop. The two cinemas here, and the café/bar/restaurant are all discussed in their relevant entries in this book.

QUEEN'S GALLERY
160 Nethergate
Tel: 01382 220660

This is Dundee's only commercial gallery for contemporary Scottish artists. Exhibitions change regularly, with around ten shows a year. Opened in 1999, the same year as DCA, they really couldn't have chosen a better time or place. It's a nice, simple space with one exposed stone wall, the rest being white painted brickwork, and it shows paintings along with small sculptures, ceramics, glasswork and jewellery – not unlike a small version of the Open Eye Gallery in Edinburgh. Shown here is the work of professional artists from all around Scotland, including Dundee of course, but also from further afield.

CINEMA

At one time, Dundee had more cinemas per capita than anywhere else in Scotland. These were wonderful palaces of entertainment, some of them furnished with marble steps and golden divans. It is with great sadness that I have to report to you that not a single one of them is still operating as a cinema. Despite the resurgence of cinema-going throughout the country, it is multiplexes that have sprouted up (the supermarkets of the cinema world), in turn closing down the lovable old picture houses. The only place to see films in the centre of Dundee is DCA. For mainstream viewing, the Odeon and UGC village-sized complexes are waiting for you on the outskirts of town. How we long for the days of the girl in the aisle with her torch and tray of ice-cream tubs with little flat wooden spatula spoons, and Kia-Ora orange . . .

DCA
Nethergate
Tel: 01382 909900

Not only is this now the only cinema in the city centre, it's also Dundee's only independent cinema, in as much as it's not an Odeon, UGC, Virgin-type place. There are two cinemas here, one with a capacity of 217, the other substantially smaller, with seating for 77. The latter shows films that aren't expected to draw such a large crowd, or that have already had their moment in Cinema One. Both show an eclectic programme of films, ranging from independent, foreign and cult movies, to the best of the mainstream offerings. Whether you're after a classic, such as *Taxi Driver*, or *Alfie*, or the newest offerings from countries as diverse as India, Japan and Norway, this is the only place to find them. Showing here are new films from the likes of David Lynch, the Coen brothers, Mike Leigh and Ken Loach (to name but a few); short seasons from particular directors, such as Jean-Luc Godard or Woody Allen; Bollywood movies; documentaries – all of which will be unlikely to show up elsewhere in town (unless they're a hot tip at the Oscars, in which case bandwagons are jumped on like there's no tomorrow). DCA Cinema also takes part in the numerous film festivals which tour the country, from the French or German festivals, to the more recent Sheffield International Documentary Film Festival. There are special movie screenings for children at weekends, with some less obvious as well as more popular offerings. This is the place to come if you truly love films and don't need a small rucksack full of rustling sweets to keep you occupied for two hours. Yes, I probably am a film snob, but I believe that going to see a film is a time when you allow yourself to switch off from the outside world and get lost in another one, just for a while. This is made a lot harder if you're surrounded by sickly smelling popcorn and folk talking all the way through, as though expecting a commercial break after 20 minutes.

An added bonus at DCA has to be the lack of hot dogs and fries for sale, although they now sell small bags of popcorn, but thankfully not the stuff that smells.

ODEON
Douglasfield
Douglas Road
Tel: 01382 504367
Information line: 0870 5050007

What can you say about the Odeon? It's a modern, purpose-built multiplex with ten screens, showing all the mainstream offerings of the week. This one at least is reachable without a car. Catch the Douglas bus (number 28 or 29) from Albert Square or at the back of the Welllgate (at the opposite side of the street). These buses are pretty frequent, and although they don't go right to the cinema door, they let you off nearby – ask your driver. Also, the numbers 15 or 17 from the town centre will drop you off at the bingo hall next door.

UGC CINEMAS
Camperdown Park
Kingsway West
Tel: 01382 828793
Information line: 0870 9020407

Again, this is a modern multi-screen mainstream cinema. It seems that if you don't have your own transport, they're really not that interested. The UGC is miles out of town, near Camperdown Park, just before you reach the Coupar Angus road. The 4a or the 4b will take you there. It's not too bad in the daytime, when these run every half hour, but in the evening, which is when you're most likely to want to go, they only run them once an hour. So, if you've just missed one, tough.

When my dad was a kid, he used to go regularly to the pictures with his mum, but times were hard and they couldn't always both afford to go. So they'd toss a coin to decide who'd go (not surprisingly, Dad always won . . .). When he came home, he'd then act out the entire film for his mum, every part, every incident. Knowing him, this re-enactment probably lasted longer than the actual film. If they were going to 'The Peak' (The Palladium) in Alexander Street, they could both afford to go, as you could get in for two 'jeely' (jam) jars. Splendid times indeed.

THEATRE

DUNDEE REP
Tay Square
Tel: 01382 223530

The first time I went to Dundee Rep, it was situated on the Lochee Road, and I went to a show there with the Brownies. All I remember is a brightly dressed and slightly scary man singing 'Lily the Pink'. Unfortunately, I'm too young to have witnessed the halcyon days when the likes of a young Glenda Jackson appeared here. It moved to its new home in Tay Square in 1982, an award-winning purpose-built theatre. Since then, many well-kent, and less-kent faces have trodden its boards. Brian Cox came back to his home city to play the lead in *The Master Builder*, and Julie T. Wallace and Joanna Lumley both appeared in *The Cherry Orchard* here. Scotland has many fine actors of its own and this is what Scottish theatre should be capitalising on.

Dundee Rep is the only professional theatre in the city. At time of writing, it operates as a traditional rep, with a full-time resident ensemble company, some of whom are in their third year here, with artistic director Hamish Glen. It has just been announced that they are to be funded for a further three years to continue with a way of working that has been seen to be a huge success. The Rep currently produces around six productions a year, with a typical season consisting of a Shakespeare play, or another classic, such as Chekhov; a couple of new pieces of writing, one usually by a local writer; a pantomime and a musical. The best recent productions, in my opinion, have been the highly praised and successful *Cabaret*, an excellent, and visually stunning production of Chekhov's *The Seagull*, directed by renowned Lithuanian director Rimas Tuminas, and *The Land o' Cakes*, the first play written by Dundee poet Don Paterson, which, although not flawless, was beautifully written for the Dundee dialect, with much well-observed humour, and lots of references to pies and cakes, which is always a good thing. The 2001 Christmas panto caused a bit of kerfuffle, when the plan to use two live rabbits in the show was met with much outcry, due to the rabbits being young, nervous and untrained. I bet they didn't have Equity cards either.

There is an insistence on producing a 'Dundee' play every year; an idea that has existed since before the ensemble company was put together. Probably the best known of these is Alan Spence's award-winning *On The Line*, which dealt with the rise and fall of Dundee's famous Timex factory in socialist Ken Loach fashion, but with a few songs thrown in. Another big hit was *The Mill Lavvies*, the highlight of which, for me anyway, were the Michael Marra-penned show numbers, including classics such as 'If Dundee was Africa' and 'There's a Big Wide World Beyond the Seedlies'. Apparently if Dundee was Africa, the Stobie would be Chad, and the Ferry would be Mozambique.

Community drama has played a big part in Dundee, most notably the groundbreaking *Witch's Blood* (1987) which involved a cast of hundreds, all from the Dundee community. It brought together writer John Harvey, and musician/songwriter Michael Marra, which was to prove a hugely successful and dynamic pairing. The audience were bussed around different sites, including Balgay Hill and the Stannergate, before being taken to Dudhope Castle for the grand finale. It was an enormous success with audiences and participants alike, and sparked off a huge demand for drama within the community.

The reputable Scottish Dance Theatre are also based at the Rep, and produce some excellent work with current artistic director Janet Smith, and some notable guest choreographers. Much of their work tours to other venues, such as the Traverse Theatre in Edinburgh.

Touring companies, both from theatre and dance, turn up at Dundee Rep on their rounds. Past guests have included Scarlett Theatre, Tag, 7:84, Boilerhouse and Yolande Snaith Dance Company. It is also the venue for annual events, such as festivals of Blues, Jazz and Guitar. Dundee Rep has also recently become the new venue for Dundee's comedy night, but at the time of writing it hasn't quite got going yet. If it works along the same lines as when it was held at The Doghouse, it should be a good night, with well-known comedians, as well as local talent, being given the chance to flex their funny bones.

There is also an excellent café/restaurant, het theatrecafé, which operates downstairs for snacks and main meals, and in the upper foyer for soup and sandwiches. (See main review p.85)

GARDYNE THEATRE
Northern College
Gardyne Road
Tel: 01382 464000

Connected to Northern College, this is a fairly basic middle-sized theatre which is used by many organisations – school productions, amateur companies such as Act IV, Tayside Opera, and productions by drama students from the HND course at Dundee College.

LITTLE THEATRE
Victoria Road

As far as I'm aware, the only company to put on productions at this tiny theatre is the long-running Dundee Dramatic Society. It hosts fairly typical am-dram fare, such as Noel Coward plays, Agatha Christie whodunnits, and Ray Coonie farces (whoops, vicar, there go my trousers . . .). They recently had proper seats installed for the first time, having used old cinema seats up until this point.

WHITEHALL THEATRE
12 Bellfield Street
Tel: 01382 434940/322684

The Whitehall is a funny old place. It's a surprisingly large old theatre and attracts an incredibly eclectic assortment of shows. Expect anything from the local Scouts' Gang Show or Junior Showtime, through to sing-a-long-a-*Sound of Music*, The Singing Kettle, and comedians such as Bill Bailey and Jerry Sadowitz. There are also a number of local amateur dramatic and operatic societies who stage productions here. Or, if you're really lucky, you might even be able to catch Paul Daniels.

LIVE MUSIC

CAIRD HALL
City Square
Booking office: 01382 434940

The late '70s and early '80s saw the Caird Hall alive with bands at least once a month, or so it seemed at the time. My first gig there was in 1979, when I went to see the Boomtown Rats (I'm not ashamed, although maybe I should be). Over the next couple of years, I must have seen about 20 bands there, who shall remain nameless – there's only so much of my past I want to reveal between these pages. There was a period through the '80s and '90s when it seemed that most major bands were missing Dundee out of their touring itineraries altogether. I'm not sure whether it's connected to the general resurgence of the city or not, but the last few years have seen a few more bands creeping back to Dundee – no one to queue up all night for, but the likes of Ocean Colour Scene and Fun Loving Criminals have turned up for the odd night. More recently, Status Quo appeared, probably doing the same gig they did here about 20 years ago – no, I wasn't there. The Caird Hall is more often used for classical concerts and opera, with many fine orchestras and companies such as RSNO, Chisinau National Orchestra and the Moscow Ballet all appearing recently. It also attracts the larger of the tribute bands, such as Bjorn Again, and some bad but popular comedians.

The smaller Marryat Hall is attached to the Caird Hall and is used for smaller concerts as well as various craft, music and antique fairs.

CHAMBERS
59–61 Gellatly Street
Tel: 01382 225616
(See 'Where to Drink' section.)

D BASEMENT
Drouthy Neebors
142 Perth Road
Tel: 01382 202187

This is a small, but good, pub venue, with an amiable atmosphere. A decent portion of it is seated, although the L-shaped room impedes viewing. It attracts mainly a young, trendy crowd and a whole bunch of different bands crop up here (no tribute bands, thankfully). There's good support here for new and local bands, as well as more established ones; d basement seems willing to support almost any music event. Previous bands include Peeps Into Fairyland, Macrocosmica (ex-Teenage Fanclub), Lateo, Mercury-Tilt Switch and Yul Peter. Apparently, Mitch the PA man is especially helpful. Gigs are usually free, or very cheap, and it's easy for young bands to promote a free mid-week gig, with the only loss risk being face rather than money.

On Fridays and Saturdays, d basement has a good DJ scene for those less inclined towards mass-market clubs.

DOGHOUSE
13 Brown Street
Tel: 01382 227080

One of the larger pub venues, the Doghouse attracts every kind of band going – local, established, tribute and cover bands. It's a good-sized space which has a capacity for around 400 people and can be partitioned off for smaller gigs. Although mostly standing room, there is some seating round the walls, and as the Doghouse has a proper raised stage, you won't encounter sightline problems, however small you are. They also have the added bonus of a decent PA system and a lighting rig. Some bands to have played recently are Gerils, Peeps Into Fairyland, Terrorvision, Lateo, Frank Black (ex-Pixies),

Delgados and Six by Seven. Depending on the act and promoter, some gigs are free, others anything up to around £8.

There's a very mixed crowd, again depending on the act, and generosity and good support for local bands from manager Ian White, which is encouraging.

DUNDEE REP
Tay Square
Tel: 01382 223530

Two or three times a year, the Rep hosts a Friday jazz night which runs for a period of six weeks at a time. Half of the restaurant (het theatrecafé) is converted into the Jazz Club venue, with both seating and standing-room downstairs, and viewing from the balcony above. It attracts a mixed crowd of swingers (no, not that kind), and a good mix of local singers and bands, as well as those from further afield. It holds around 150 downstairs, and a variable amount upstairs, although it does sometimes get quite crowded. Tickets cost around £4, with discounts available. If you've been in for some delicious food first, and buy a ticket for the Jazz Club, you can keep your excellent viewing position should you wish to make a night of it. A good time is guaranteed.

Other local bands play occasionally, and there are yearly jazz and blues festivals, with Dundee's independently run Guitar festival usually choosing the Rep as the venue for their annual outing too. Check the Rep brochure and local press for up-to-date info.

FAT SAM'S
31 South Ward Road
Tel: 01382 228181

A club venue that occasionally attracts bands. Ash and Bjorn Again are the only recent ones that spring to mind. They host yearly Battle

PUB DOGS

A pub dog is a great feature in any pub, and it's high time there was a category for them at Crufts. Here are a few locals I met on my travels.

GLEN

The ultimate pub dog, Glen has been a regular of the Clep for 15 years, and now visits every afternoon. Prefers to bring his own snacks.

RIGGS

Riggs has a civilised routine of popping in to the Royal Arch for coffee every morning before his beach walk. Also enjoys bottled Miller, and has his own bowl behind the bar.

TOOTS
Our cover dog, Toots is pictured here in the Campbeltown Bar. She likes Mini Cheddars dipped in Bailey's Irish Cream.

ALFIE
Book mascot Alfie is seen here in the Phoenix Bar. They don't actually allow dogs inside but being one of my favourite pubs, it seemed right and proper to bring them together.

The Pillars

Phoenix Bar

The Agacan

Taybridge Bar

Land o' cakes

Zeme ż lezák

Triffles . . .

. . . Pehs and Bridies

Sutherlands window

Alastair Jamieson's window

Smallest corner shop in the world

Lobster holiday

of the Bands, the prize for which is the chance to play at T in the Park.

ON AIR EAST
15 Ward Road
Tel: 01382 203226

Formerly known as The Mission, and this will probably soon also be 'formerly On Air East'. They have hosted some good gigs, including the very fine Willard Grant Conspiracy, JJ72, Jackie Leven, Clinic and My Vitriol. The future, though, looks bleak.

WESTPORT BAR
22 East Henderson's Wynd
Tel: 01382 200993

Upstairs at the Westie is one of Dundee's most-used small music venues. Traditionally a musos' pub, due to various connections with ex-Danny Wilson members, and the Clark family in general. Although Scotty is now at Mickey Coyle's, the Westie still has a loyal clientele, with Dundee musos split between the two. Music-wise, expect all types of bands to appear here, from professionally promoted gigs, to local kids trying themselves out for size. As with many music venues these days, tribute bands show up most weeks. Over the years, this venue has been host to Swiss Family Orbison, Bis, Teenage Fanclub, Jah Wobble, Selector, Lateo (they get around), Long Fin Killie, and the very fine Michael Marra, who once did a gig up here with Liz Lochhead. Depending on the band, entrance fees vary from very cheap, to around £8 for bigger names. It holds 100 max, but even with 50 it looks busy. Apart from a handful of chairs, it's standing only, so if you're small, stand near the front. The Westport Bar is friendly, and provides good support for local bands. (It's also available for private hire – parties, discos, etc.)

CLUBS

Clubs, traditionally, are for drinking Scotch on the rocks and smoking cigars, with maybe the strains of a jazz trumpeter heard through the smoke. Back then, if it was dancing you were after, you went to a disco. This has become a laughable term, and you will be made to feel about 20 years out of date if you were to – God forbid – suggest going to a 'disco'. Dancing is now done in 'nightclubs', usually known simply as 'clubs', and you don't go 'dancing' any more, one goes 'clubbing'. Presumably from the verb, 'to club'. It all sounds very neanderthal to me. Didn't cavemen club their women and drag them back to their cave for a bit of procreation? Perhaps they too went out in large groups, intent on going clubbing. So, things haven't changed that much after all. But I digress. Whatever you want to call it, 'club' is currently the accepted term for a place that plays music loudly, with the provision of a dancefloor should you wish to move your body in response to it. So – here we have . . . clubs.

Right. This is where things get a bit sticky. I like to drink in pubs, eat in restaurants, and shop in shops, so feel I can give a fair judgement of these places. I don't, however, partake in the club thing. It's not that I'm a party pooper, but the music generally played in clubs at weekends – which, let's face it, is the best time to dance – just doesn't tap my shoes. I have relied on trusted voices and idle gossip to inform me (and therefore you) as to what the low-down is regarding the strobed and mirror-balled dance emporiums of Dundee. I hope this will give you a fair idea of what to expect, although one party-girl's club experience will be quite different from the next. Also, there are so many different 'nights' happening, that these will probably have changed by the time you read this. Posters and flyers are always around to inform of the latest goings-on though. So, get on your dancing shoes and sequinned bikini, and let's go to clubland.

THE CIRCUS
Meadowside (former Post Office)
Tel: 0870 7572913

The Circus has come to town. So says the pre-publicity campaign anyway. This is the most recent addition to Dundee's club scene, and the only one I've personally visited in many a year. It didn't happen out of choice – I'd been on a work night out, and some folk fancied going on to a club. I have to say I was extremely reluctant as, despite a love of dancing, as I've said, I'm not really a club girl. However, I foolishly allowed myself to be convinced that it would be good research for the book. Tuesday seemed a safe-ish night to go; I thought I might even have a dance – weekdays in clubland are well known for playing 'retro' stuff ('70s disco and funk, etc.). Thus I found myself at The Circus. Having paid a reasonable £2.50 to get in, we were then informed it was 'Shag Tag' night. Oh joy of joys. Apparently, the idea is that you wear your number (686 – how can I forget?) and if a fellow 'tagger' fancies you, they write up theirs and your numbers on the 'Shag' board, and you decide if you want to mate on the dancefloor. Shag Tag is very much a student union thing, and with most clubs having student nights, I suppose it's no surprise that they've 'tagged' along, so to speak. The Circus is a huge place, with lots of bars of varying sizes, and an ample dancefloor. Unfortunately, everything about me was wrong for the place (or is that the other way around?) – hair too short, skirt too long, top too high, shoes too low, tights too thick, skin too thin . . .

There's a VIP lounge, and I tried to ascertain the purpose of this and how you could get in, etc., but I didn't quite get to the bottom of it. Perhaps their numbers were printed, rather than written in felt-tip pen . . . who knows? I managed to get lost in the ladies' loo too – not due to excess alcohol consumption, I hasten to add, but because of the bizarre layout of this enormous peeing emporium. I didn't investigate, but it looked as though there was yet another bar adjoining the loos. I felt a bit like Alice in Wonderland, and wondered whether I would ever enter the real world again. After a bit of navigation (compasses available from the girl at the kiosk selling hairspray, tights, etc.) I found my way back into the world of Shag Tag. Some student 'games' were part of the entertainment, in between some half-decent music. I left around 2.30 a.m. with my ears ringing like they haven't rung since that Motorhead gig back in 1981 – and with me concluding that I'm now, officially, old. Oh well, at least I tried.

ENIGMA
4–6 South Ward Road
Tel: 01382 200066

This is pretty much your standard city-centre club tucked away behind the main Ward Road thoroughfare in an old warehouse space. Beyond the purple paintwork and metallic studded doors you will find three bars, a modest-sized dancefloor and a seated 'chill' space upstairs. Club sounds range from a variety of hard house through the week to a more chart-orientated selection on Saturdays – brought to the punters by a variety of current touring DJs. Themed nights occur on a regular basis, including Old School Reunion Nights playing '90s dancefloor sounds and there's an ice-cream van in the courtyard to cool down the under-age clubbers.

FAT SAM'S
31 South Ward Road
Tel: 01382 228181

Once upon a time, Fat Sam's, or 'Fatties' as it's affectionately known, was considered to be the best nightclub in the whole of Scotland. It's been around for years, and I think the last time I was there was around ten years ago when the Wedding Present played a gig there. It's still a gig venue, but mostly it's a club. It's split into two sections – the main dance area, which gets very busy and very hot and sweaty, and the large 'cocktail bar' which you can retire to for chilling-out purposes. Apparently, a large amount of the chatting-up happens in here too. At time of writing, Wednesdays had a healthy mix of soul, funk and R & B for funking down to; Thursday nights were indie, rock and alt. night; Friday nights included '70s funk, as well as house and garage, and Saturdays were – well – Saturdays, with mainly techno, house and trance, and a large amount of dry ice to get your thirst up, and the weight of your wallet down. Fatties generally attracts a slightly older crowd than most of the other clubs (i.e. the lads have started shaving).

HOMELESS
(Currently on the move, due to end up at Foundation, Blackscroft, sometime soon)

Homeless is a club with no home, that takes up residence in other venues, and sets up events wherever possible. As long as it has a home, Homeless happens every week, with 'resident' DJs, Eat Not Sold, as well as respected guest DJs from around the country. There's a mix of hip-hop, drum and bass, and some soul funk. It's very popular and busy, with a friendly atmosphere. Prices vary from around a fiver to about £12, depending on the night.

Homeless has moved from On Air East to Club Cruise (behind Oxygen), and is soon to be squatting in Foundation on Blackscroft. Not so much homeless as nomadic.

LIBERTY'S
124 Seagate
Tel: 01382 200660

I read somewhere that Liberty's is the largest and most successful gay and lesbian nightclub on the east coast of Scotland. I can't vouch for this, but it's certainly pretty popular, and is cheaper than most other clubs in town. Open five nights a week, from Wednesdays to Sundays, it plays a mix of commercial, garage and house.

MARDI GRAS
21 South Ward Road
Tel: 01382 205551

The Mardi has rapidly become one of Scotland's most successful commercial nightclubs since opening its doors in 1995. Between then and now, it's increased its capacity for sweaty dancers to 1200, and has two dancing cages for the more shy, retiring types. It has a bit of a reputation as a pick-up joint, which doesn't seem exceptional in the world of clubbing, and I'm sure is fine if that's the purpose of your night out. Open every night, the Mardi has a varied menu of dance nights. At the time of writing, Wednesday was student night, with an eclectic bunch of stuff from pop to dance to indie. Thursdays were similar, with stuff from '70s, '80s and '90s – and on Fridays and Saturdays you get what you would expect from a large commercial club, with Saturday being cited as 'Dundee's Big Night Out'. There's lots of typical chart dance with some house thrown in, and 'music to get off with girls to', playing as they do appropriate smoochy numbers. A fairly mainstream place in club terms, and huge.

OASIS
St Andrews Lane
Tel: 01382 221061

Oasis publicity states, 'If you're not over 25, you're not cool enough to go'. Open from Thursday to Saturday, every night they play dance tunes from the '60s to the '90s. At a guess, I'd say that most folk who come here are well over 25.

OXYGEN
60 Brown Street
Tel: 01382 200299

Tucked away in the back streets, Oxygen has a host of resident and guest DJs, two rooms, and three bars. Expect mainly techno, with the odd jungle and house night. Wednesdays are student nights.

RATTRAY'S
1a Rattray Street
Tel: 01382 202303

Here they play garage, breakbeat and house on Fridays, and 'Deep 'n' Dirty' on Saturdays, with hard house going pretty much all night. It's bigger than it looks on the outside, and very smoky.

HISTORIC, SIGHTSEEING AND OTHER GOOD THINGS TO DO

BROUGHTY FERRY CASTLE
Castle Approach
Tel: 01382 436916

Broughty Ferry Castle is now a quirky wee museum which sits next to the harbour, with the sandy beach to one side and the stony one to the other. I hadn't visited since I was quite young, so didn't really know what was in store. On entering, I climbed a tight inner spiral staircase. The first floor is devoted to the history of Broughty Ferry, with pictures of old paddle-steamers that used to ferry people between here and Tayport; the history of the lifeboat, with models and relevant paraphernalia, and a lovely old map of the area. Back into the wee stairwell and it's up to the second floor, which celebrates Dundee's whaling days. This rather gory exhibition has some pretty interesting stuff, including a seaman's ditty box, a jar of whale oil, and various killing devices used through the ages. Once the whale's dead, the old blubber spade and flensing knife get put into action (flensing is the removal of blubber from a whale's body) – these too are on display. It's all very sad, but I suppose that was life in the old days. The most modern of the harpoon devices on display was equipped with an explosive grenade, so essentially the whale was internally blown up. Nice.

There are some good pictures of Eskimos, and one of a Dundee whaler marooned somewhere called Disco Island, although there didn't seem to be much of a party going on. I also saw a whale's eardrum, and a selection of scrimshaw, including a very sweet carved Brancussi-esque penguin. On one wall hangs a fairly dreadful painting of some ships and penguins and a lot of ice.

The tight stair beckons again, and I found myself on the third floor, which is the Wildlife and Seashore department. I was met by Nipper the Crab who introduces you to a selection of shells and their former occupants. A fairly unimpressive tank of plastic fish is topped with a couple of stuffed gulls, who are much smaller than the ones outside McDonald's. Then I moved on to Tideline Treasure, which consists of some agates and pebbles stuck onto bits of card. More impressive are the two glass cabinets of polished agates, amethysts and quartz.

Moving swiftly up to the fourth floor, I found more stuffed birds, rather incongruously next to The Defence of the Tay section. This is basically the history of the part Broughty Ferry has played in defending Dundee through the ages. There's a nice bunch of spurs and swords, most notably a sixteenth-century claymore, and some rather fetching basket-hilt broadswords. A small cabinet is dedicated to the Boer War, with assorted memorabilia, including souvenir pottery, a Queen Victoria tin of chocolates, and an anonymous quote which reads 'We don't want to fight, but by jingo if we do, we've got the ships, we've got the men, we've got the money too.' By jingo, indeed.

One of the lovely things about this quaint castle/museum is that on each floor you can look out of the windows in various directions, giving great views across the beach and river, to Monifieth, Buddon Ness, and Tentsmuir, without the icy wind tearing through your ears. The observation area on the top level also gives good views, and informs you what you're looking at, in case you hadn't worked out where the beach was. A wee shop on the first floor will sell you the usual souvenir rulers, toffee, etc.

DISCOVERY/DISCOVERY POINT
Discovery Quay
Tel: 01382 201245

Since it was returned to the city in 1986, Dundee has capitalised big-time on the attraction of having a big ship to show off, subsequently claiming itself to be the 'City of Discovery'. If I see one more business calling itself 'Discovery' something or other, I'll scream. We already have Discovery Windows, Taxis, Gas, Roofing, Security, Computing, Ceilings . . . need I go on? It's not as comical as 'What's it called? Cumbernauld', but it has given rise to many jokes about what there is to discover in Dundee, other than this ship itself. It was built in Dundee in 1901, and Captain Scott went off on one of his icy expeditions aboard the *Discovery* and duly got himself stuck in the ice. The whole story is unfolded for you at the Discovery Centre. It had been some eight years since I'd visited, but one of the things I remembered enjoying was the recreated cross-section of part of the ship, showing how she would have been built. When I visited recently, this area of the centre was closed, and was undergoing some refits and modifications, but it will be reopened by summer 2002.

A screening of 'Trapped in the Ice' was about to start, so I was whizzed through to watch this. There are three mobile screens which swivel, shift and open out as the *Discovery's* story is told. The climax comes when the ship is freed from the ice, and she bursts through the screens in triumph, although the ship is actually the *Terra Nova*. Oh well. Back to the temporary starting point, where display boards inform you about the crew – how they entertained themselves in total darkness 24 hours a day (ice football, apparently), and what they wore (check out the wooden snow goggles). Also, there's a very long pair of skis and a rather unpleasant photo of a frostbitten hand. (Ouch.) The dark wood-panelled walls add an appropriate shippy atmosphere.

At this point, you would usually see the film, but we've been there already – so it's through to the scientific research exhibition. Set-ups with figures going about their chilly research against some rather lumpen ice/snow backdrops make up this section, with a display cabinet containing a stuffed penguin. (Apparently Wilson the zoologist was forever skinning the little blighters on deck, but was said to have a deep love of nature.) Then we shiver through to the 'Forgotten Years', a slide show above a mock-up of the sea – and then to some mini displays on magnetism, strength, and other scientific stuff.

The exhibitions are all interesting, but at the end of the day, the ship's the thing, and once outside, I was more than ready to go on board. Much restoration has taken place, but you get a great feel for what she might have been like some 100 years ago. Down below where the workers would be is suitably rugged – apparently their bath rota meant that they only got a bath once every 47 days, but with the minus-70 temperatures, you probably wouldn't notice the smell. On your way down, you'll bump into a couple of very sooty men shovelling coal, and lots of creaky noises, which made me think we were about to set sail any moment.

Past some provision crates (carrots, sprouts, etc.) and panting beams, I felt like I was in another world, until I stumbled upon a circular perspex 'Sounds of the Antarctica' display, which spoiled my romantic notions of being a sailor.

I was enjoying my salty dog experience, so I went back up some polished wooden stairs with shiny brass handrails, and found myself in the kitchen – sorry – 'gantry'. There I saw a stuffed cat, and a chef with a big nose cooking up some delights, with the washing-up still in the sink. Next, it's through to the mess deck (the living and sleeping quarters for most of the crew), and then it all became much more civilised when I reached the officers' mess. A beautiful long wooden table and some chairs (screwed to the floor), take centre stage. The officers' private rooms, which you can nosy into, line the outside.

Back up on deck, I found myself alone and with a sudden longing for distant shores. However, this ship wasn't going anywhere, so I stepped back onto dry land, and returned to Discovery Point and into the land of Polarama, an interactive Antarctica – how big, how cold, how dry, how windy . . . Also there are videos showing seals and musical icebergs, microscopes for looking at slides of bed bugs and the like, and a food-chain pyramid – all brilliant fun for children.

Discovery has a large shop, which sells predictable Discovery gear, as well as shortbread, books, t-shirts and jam. It also has a reasonable café, although they don't sell ship's biscuits.

MILLS OBSERVATORY
Glamis Road
Balgay Park
Tel: 01382 435846

Dundee is very lucky to have its own public observatory, the only one in the country with a resident astronomer. It has a domed roof, which somewhat bizarrely is made of papier-mâché. Once inside, you will find display boards on all the planets and some quirky exhibits, such as a model of Buzz Aldrin walking on the moon, planting his American flag, with his tinfoil Apollo 11 behind him. Upstairs, there are displays of Tayside's astronomers and some gorgeous old telescopes, one made by Dundee's own celebrated instrument maker, George Lowdon. A beautiful old circular wooden seat takes centre-stage here, and you can go outside and become a human sundial, or take in the breathtaking views across to Fife. Back inside is the telescope room and planetarium, which is only open for viewing at certain times with the resident astronomer. When I visited, it was the wrong time for this and they were also in-between astronomers, but I believe it's all quite spectacular. The best time for viewing is in winter. The attendants are enthusiastic and friendly and know their stuff, so there's always someone on hand to answer your questions. Unless you have a car, it's a bit tricky visiting after dark, which is obviously the best time to see the stars. Being in the middle of a large park and at the top of a hill, I wouldn't recommend walking up here at night, unless you're ten feet tall, covered in hair, and have a ferocious growl. You'll need to either find a friend with a car, or hire a taxi. It's not very well sign-posted until you're nearly there, by which time you know you're nearly there anyway. Worth making the effort for.

OLD STEEPLE
City Churches
Overgate
Tel: 01382 206790

Scotland's highest surviving medieval tower was closed during the period I hoped to visit. Fortunately my niece had visited the previous year, and imparted some of her thoughts to me. What she remembers most is that it attracted American tourists, who she took to be vampires, as they kept insisting that they had to get back to their hotel before sunset (shouldn't that be sunrise?). When pressed, she did manage to tell me that she'd had a good time, that the views were great (especially on a clear day), and that the guides were interesting. You can see all round Dundee from up here, and across the river to Fife and beyond, although it can be a bit windy. She also remembers being shown where prisoners were held before being beheaded in the tower or hanged in the Overgate – and other gory tales. The sort of stuff that nice young girls like. One of the best things about the Old Steeple is that you get to see a fully operational belfry – worth making a trip to the top for. Apparently, the original bells cracked due to over-enthusiastic bell-ringing when Bonnie Prince Charlie's dad visited the city. A tour of the tower (which translates as 'a tour of the tour' in Dundonian) lasts approximately 45 minutes.

HM FRIGATE *UNICORN*
Victoria Dock
Tel: 01382 200900

The *Unicorn* doesn't have the splendour or the financial input of the *Discovery*, but she is such an endearingly simple old frigate that I took to her immediately. This is the oldest British-built warship still afloat, and I've been told that at one time she was turned into a hospital ship, which would explain why she looks more like a large barge than a sailing ship. On the top deck, the best place to start your visit, there are a number of models, showing how she would have looked in her prime, all sails-a-flapping. The models are great – look out for one in particular where the figurehead looks more like a curious donkey-dog. A number of battleship-grey painted display cabinets contain some lovely old memorabilia, including a Norwegian foghorn, although sadly most exhibits are without labels, so you're left to invent your own stories about them. There's also a series of wooden carved ribbons with the ship's battle honours, and the ship's wheel which is enormous – it's hard to imagine anyone being able to turn such a thing.

Back down on the gun deck, I liked how randomly everything was laid out; the whole ship has less of a museum feel than other similar attractions. In amongst this, are some rather dodgy cut-out figures of sailors with mugs of ale and large earrings, who all look like they're up to no good. A series of very large, original cannons are lined up along one side, with a display of various types of cannon shot. There's also a lovely example of a pulling gig (an old wooden racing boat). The captain's cabin is on this deck, and has two dwarf-sized squint doors which give it a fairytale feel.

Down the trepidous steps (careful now) and we're down on the mess deck, which has a very low ceiling – even I had to mind my head. Here you'll find cabins, hammocks, some huge barrels, and displays of sailmaking tools – huge copper nails and marlin spikes. There are also some randomly placed pieces of white painted plywood displaying various tools such as three splendid crosscut saws. Along one side are wooden tables, slung from the ceiling by ropes. One is laid out with jugs, etc., with a very sorry-looking soul, looking much the worse for wear and showing much evidence of scurvy or frostbite.

For me, the highlight, and real treat, was going down even further to the orlop deck. Now, I'm not very tall and I was bent double walking around down here. That might not be your idea of fun, but it was fantastic. You're right in the bowels of the ship here and as you practically crawl your way along narrow corridors it's like a big adventure, and for me, it was more exciting than the *Discovery*. At one point you even come across a treasure trunk. This lowest deck is the ship's storage area, and is the part of her which is the most original.

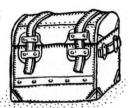

The *Unicorn* is a quiet, modest ship who doesn't blow her own bosun's whistle. There's something very authentic about her – the smells, the original wood – and although many of the exhibits are shabby and look as though they may never have seen better days, the beauty and attraction is in the ship herself, rather than what's been added to her. Sadly lacking in financial support, the *Unicorn* deserves much more attention than she presently gets. She is available to hire for parties, weddings and events. Highly recommended.

VERDANT WORKS
West Henderson's Wynd
Tel: 01382 225282

Even if you're not from Dundee, it's unlikely you won't know about the city's jute industry. I won't get all historical on you, as there's plenty of stuff out there already. I must admit though, I thought I was going to find this visit a bit dull, but am glad to say my presumptions were wrong. This award-winning heritage centre has been extremely well put together, and will give you a great insight into the whole jute thing, from growing the stuff to the many diverse uses of the end product. A wee cinema shows a 15-minute narrated film and gives a brief introduction to Dundee and its juteness. You're now ready for your jute journey. You will be led through the first part by one of the informative volunteer guides. A particularly impressive part is the office, with all its original mahogany furniture and fittings. It is exactly as it would have been during its working life. Right. Now you're on your own to explore the plantations of India, admire some bales of jute, and hear voice-overs of grunting men loading the ships. A map of the world shows you where jute has been used, and what it's been used for (ventilating mine shafts in Australia was a new one to me). Past the mid-nineteenth-century hand loom and muckle wheel (official name), and you get a chance to steer your own clipper. I chose to go to Australia with 20 jute machines, but somehow ended up in Jamaica. Geography was never my strong point . . . Next it's through to a large room with examples of all the machines used in jute production. They're scaled-down versions of the ones actually used in factories, but they are probably as noisy. Again, volunteers are on hand to put the machines into action. From roving to beaming to spinning, it's all here. The weaving machine is very noisy and looks quite vicious. I left clutching my wee piece of woven jute, given to me by my cheery machine operator. Phew. There's still more to come – lots of interactive stuff about sign language, etc.; examples of Jenny-spinners and rope machines; and a contemporary section showing modern uses for jute, flax and its plastic cousin, polypropylene. Don't miss the portable machine for testing the moisture of your jute – in fact, never leave home without one. Then there's a section on the Indian jute industry – us going over there, making a good few bucks and getting them to do all the work, basically. You then move swiftly through to Jute Fashion, which includes a Mary Quant jute skirt (thick tights recommended). There's much to see, read and do here and it's all excellently presented, with enough text to inform you without wearing you down – but, there's more . . .

Upstairs there are various displays of the more social aspect of Dundee around this time and health issues are illustrated with some unpleasantries – such as a tooth key for DIY teeth pulling. There are also more voice-overs telling of general surrounding squalor and reproduction photos of various social activities. You can also experience a plettie (see 'Dundee Dialect' section), if you've never been on a real one. I really enjoyed my visit to Verdant Works, and am saddened by its current financial difficulties. It would be a crying shame if this slice of Dundee history were to go under. I do feel the entrance fee is a little high, and location-wise it's a bit tucked away, but the fact that it's in the heart of an industrial area is part of the beauty of this working museum.

Like all good tourist attractions, it has its own shop, which sells a bizarre range of goods, from the usual 'Verdant' pencils and rulers, through to Mrs Bridge's Lemon Curd, and whoopee cushions. Thankfully, there's also a coffee shop attached (I needed a rest after my excursion). It's very friendly and cheap; a tasty toastie and coffee for around £2, and some very home-made cakes which reminded me of coffee mornings.

OTHER GOOD THINGS TO DO

BOTANIC GARDEN
Burnaby Street (off Riverside Drive)
Tel: 01382 566939

Quietly tucked away at the west end of the Perth Road, behind imposing mansion houses to its north and a steep cliff edge overlooking the Tay to its south, are Dundee's Botanic Gardens. Established in 1971 to supply plant material for research purposes, it's now known as 'the jewel in the crown' of Dundee University. This south-sloping 9.5 hectare garden site comfortably nestles into its own sunny microclimate and is an ideal way to spend a Sunday afternoon, with good manageable walks. On entering the gardens you are greeted by the modernist geometry of the Visitors' Centre, contrasting against the foliage with its stark lines of white concrete, black timber and glazed screens. The interior creates an interesting procession of spaces with a small exhibition area and a friendly café which serves up simple fare, such as toasties, soup and baked tatties. Immediately to the left of the Visitors' Centre is a large glasshouse that houses both tropical and temperate environments, with a small but increasing selection of exotic plants – watch out for the 'jungle' pond with giant lilies, and a beautiful selection of tropical climbers. The main garden runs on an east–west axis and takes you through a variety of habitats, including a large ornamental pond, a formal herb garden, a woodland area with wildlife pond and a developing rocky moorland terrain. As you wander through this extensive selection of British and world plant species, with the backdrop of a number of wonderful Arts & Crafts and Scots Renaissance mansions, it can often seem that you may be trespassing on some well-travelled jute baron's land. On my last visit, whilst keeping an eye open for that imaginary gamekeeper, I particularly liked the imposing array of conifers, the beautiful eucalyptus trees and the paper-bark textures on the birch collection. I think one of the great things about this garden is that you can come back again and again and always discover something new, due to seasonal variations – whether it's the arrival of the Himalayan poppy blooms around the ornamental pond in the summer, or the wonderful riot of colour created by the autumn leaves.

In the summer the gardens also hosts music events, workshops and plant sales. They are open throughout the year and at the time of writing the admission price was £1.50.

CAMPERDOWN PARK AND WILDLIFE CENTRE
Coupar Angus Road
Tel: 01382 432661

This is Dundee's largest park and is the furthest from the city centre. It's not hugely accessible without your own transport, but the number 18 and 19 buses will take you within around 10–15 minutes' walk of the main entrance. Within its 395 acres, there are a lot of open spaces, rare trees – including the famous and beautiful Camperdown Elm – and some impressive rhododendrons. If you're lucky, you may stumble across pieces of public art, including Chris Biddlecombe's *Eight-Person Kissing Compass*, which uses local stone and wood to create sculptural 'kissing' seats, with pointers to the areas around the park. Also in Camperdown Park, there are tennis courts, a boating pond, horse riding, an adventure playground, and an 18-hole championship golf course.

Camperdown Wildlife Centre is home to a number of captive animals from Britain and Europe. Pigs and hens are neighbours to brown bears, wolves, lynxes and Scottish wildcats. They also have a golden eagle, some deer and a big shed full of creepy crawlies, if you like that sort of thing.

At the top end of the golf course is Camperdown House, a lovely neoclassical house built in 1828, which has had much of its splendour ripped out. It is currently closed for renovation, so hopefully they may be restoring some of this.

SENSATION
Greenmarket
DD1 4QB
Tel: 01382 228800

Do you know your cochlea from your semi-circular canals? Did you know that grasshoppers hear with their knees? All this, and much more is revealed at Sensation, Dundee's science centre. It seems obvious now and it's with a certain amount of embarrassment that I have to admit that I hadn't clicked with the play on words thing. Given that the word 'sense', if you elongate the 'eh' sound so that it's pronounced 'seh-ense', is Dundonian for science, maybe it's not such a common mistake around here. In truth, it *is* a science centre, but the whole thing is based around the senses (of course). Sensation is a completely hands-on centre aimed at children, with zones for each of the five senses. The main area is filled with 'posts' where you learn about smelling, hearing, etc. Different species are compared, with the shrew putting in a number of appearances. I went on a Wednesday afternoon and there was no one else around, so I entertained myself with a bit of keyhole surgery, watched myself turn into an old woman, sat inside a very large eyeball, and tried on a pair of elephant's ears. Unfortunately I was too tall to play with the enormous head – into which you climb through the nostril, slide past the area where snot's made, and come shooting out onto the tongue.

It's all bright and chunky and many of the large models have a charming, homespun quality to them, a bit like classroom projects that have got out of hand, and all the information is painted on by hand. One of these that I particularly liked was the fibreglass model of skin, magnified 1,000 times; when you walk around one side, you're faced with an enormous spot, a blackhead, and a whitehead. Sadly, the interaction stops here, and you don't get to squeeze them. You can, however, walk inside the skin to see what it's like under the surface. There are a number of pieces where you look at yourself on a TV screen. One puts up a thermal image of your teeth, which change colour as you breathe. The result is a cross between a black-and-white minstrel and Papa Lazarou from the *League of Gentlemen*.

Although the look of Sensation is geared towards younger children, each zone has information cards called 'hard stuff', which is aimed at older kids. One activity definitely for the older ones is the Gyro Gym, a contraption that you're caged into and spun around to varying degrees of disorientation. I'm told it's great fun, but not in a scary way.

There's heaps of stuff to do here, whether you want to test yourself for colour blindness, play the pheromone game (where boy moth meets girl moth), or find out what the hairs in your nose are for (yes, we all have them) – you're guaranteed to learn something new.

Plant life is also explained, with another 'magnified 1,000 times' model, this time of a leaf. Kids can climb in through the stalk and learn about chlorophyll and the like. The 'see the world as a dog/bird/fish' areas are possibly the least successful. In the bird one, you look through four wee windows cut into the floor, which allow you to look down on some rather makeshift revolving models of houses and trees, etc. Most alarming to me – let alone the bird whose view we were taking on – was the duck, which was the size of a small housing estate.

Overall, Sensation doesn't have the dynamism you would usually associate with a science centre, being more low-tech than high-tech, but it's a lot of fun, especially for children. It's a people-friendly space and is busy at weekends and during the school holidays.

Upstairs is a café, a technosphere surf zone (where you can surf for free), and an education room. On the ground floor is the statutory shop, which sells – as well as the usual pencil sharpeners and keyrings – chemistry sets, microscopes, anatomically correct human-torso kits, and even a recording studio. A fine place to take the kids on a rainy Sunday afternoon.

SHAWS DUNDEE SWEET FACTORY
The Keillers Buildings
34 Mains Loan
Tel: 01382 461435

This is a proper working sweet factory where you get the opportunity to witness grown men wrestling with large slabs of toffee, and striping your humbugs (these demonstrations are not on over the winter period). It may not have the madness of Charlie and the Chocolate Factory but it still has loads of appeal and is great fun. Sweets are made in the traditional way in big copper pans and there's a large shop where you can buy all your old favourites. Summer is the best time to go, as they're open Monday to Friday. In spring and autumn opening times are reduced to Wednesday afternoons only. The shop is still open the rest of the week. Best to check times before you go, and don't forget to brush your teeth after all that sweetie sampling.

STOBSMUIR POND
Stobsmuir Park
Pitkerro Road
(Heading north, after Baxter Park, but before Stobswell Park)

Known as the 'swanny pond', on account of its resident swans, you can take a wee rowing boat out here in the summer months. It's not very deep though, so watch you don't keep hitting the bottom with your oars. Handier to get to without a car than Camperdown Park.

4

Where to Shop

Dundee city centre is extremely compact and has the added benefit of being largely pedestrianised. The Wellgate and Overgate shopping centres mark the two end points of the mainstream shopping experience, linked as they are by the High Street and Murraygate. There's nothing remarkable to report along this stretch, with the usual High Street stores jostling for your attention – Marks and Spencer, Top Shop, Next . . . fill in the blanks.

I'm not much of a fan of shopping centres, but the new Overgate is worthy of a mention architecturally, if not for its mundane chain stores. Formerly a hideous carbuncle of the first degree, the 1960s Overgate was mercifully demolished, and not before time. The building that has replaced it has attracted stores which previously wouldn't have given Dundee the time of day. The decision to leave one side of the centre free of shops and instead have an entire wall of glass running not only from one end of the building to the other, but from ceiling to floor, has worked stunningly well. At last, Dundee's City Churches, with the medieval tower, are given centre stage in a corner of the city which has been blighted with bad planning. (Apparently, when the horror story that became the previous Overgate was in planning, the demolition of the City Churches was discussed, as it was felt the building wouldn't be in keeping with their modern, forward-thinking designs. Scary.) Just as importantly, the abundance of glass here also results in this consumer's palace being filled with natural light, which makes it feel like an enclosed, sheltered street. This makes a nice change from the more typical claustrophobic, faceless, warren-like shopping malls which are completely enclosed, giving little or no indication of time or place. It's still a shopping mall though. The best of the shop crop are: Fopp (record shop), H&M, and The Natural World – which are nestled amongst the more ubiquitous offerings such as Next, Gap and a very large Debenhams. There's also a USC shop with the usual range of designer labels, some of the better ones being the less showy Firetrap and Stark.

The Wellgate, sadly, is struggling to keep up, having been abandoned by several stores. The main attractions here are Virgin and Woolworth's. On the top floor, the former Wellgate Market/Inshops is now home to TK Maxx, (known in Dundee as 'Tinky Max'), a glory-hole for bargain hunters. Starbucks have recently opened one of their millions of coffee shops in the Wellgate in a bid to perk things up.

The city centre has a number of small side streets which leave more room for the individual outlets. In Castle Street alone, you can buy a made-to-measure kilt, an espresso machine, Arbroath smokies, a telescope or a grand piano, while in Commercial Street, there's nothing to stop you from buying yourself some smoked tofu, a Mexican wardrobe, a pair of swimming goggles, or a copy of Basil Brush's biography.

SPECIALIST SHOPS – FOOD AND DRINK

Bakeries and Cakeries

For a city with such a pie-eating populace, it shouldn't come as a surprise to find such an abundance of bakeries in Dundee. What is surprising is the quality. Whether it's pies, cakes or bread you're after, Dundee won't disappoint. Fisher & Donaldson is most certainly the stop for the more discerning cake buyer; Goodfellow & Steven's is a perfect stepping stone for those not ready for the upper echelons of F&D; Wallace's, more famous for their pies and bridies, are popular suppliers of the more trusty fare. Certain areas of Dundee have a plethora of wee indie bakeries – Albert Street and Hilltown are two notable stretches of dough worship. For that late-night starch refuelling, one of Dundee's all-night bakeries should do the trick.

FISHER & DONALDSON
12 Whitehall Street; 300 Perth Road; 83 High Street, Lochee

Founded in 1919 in St Andrews, Fisher & Donaldson describes itself as 'the premier baker of the East of Scotland' and it probably is. This is the crème de la crème of bakeries. I challenge anyone to walk past its creamy windows of strawberry tarts and fondant fancies without having the tiniest peek at their wares. Their prices are higher than other Dundee cakeries, but they're worth it. From the simple Belgian biscuit and Selkirk bannock, to the coveted coffee towers and the more elaborate gateaux, F&D know how to tickle your tastebuds. They also sell some of the finest bread you can buy – Dr Floyd's seeded batch. At around £1.10 a loaf, you won't want to waste a single sesame seed, but it's the king of the bread world. F&D also sell their own hand-made chocolates, tins of shortbread and the legendary Dundee cake. They also sell pies – but quite posh ones, including the very dainty 'supper pie' and one made with lamb and mint.

The Whitehall Street and Perth Road branches also have a café attached (see p.96) which serves a decent cuppa. It's no good if you're on a diet, though – even if your intention is to simply have a cup of coffee or tea, you'll be tempted . . . I believe, however, that we all need treats now and again. So go on, spoil yourself.

GOODFELLOW & STEVEN
24 Union Street; 193 Albert Street; 173 Perth Road; 83 Gray Street, Broughty Ferry

I always associate Goodfellow & Steven with birthday cakes and chocolate violets. Our family birthday celebrations weren't complete without the reassuring words 'I got you a cake from Goodies'. I never ate the chocolate violets as I thought they would taste of flowers, but they were always in Goodies' window, and a friend's mum used to send them abroad to a relative, who missed them so much. They're still sold in boxes of six.

The biggest of the G&S bakers in Dundee is actually in Broughty Ferry, which also has the Café Vienna attached. This is by far the most glamorous of the branches, with a large window display and long counter. There are a number of smaller branches in Dundee, as well as further afield, in the likes of Montrose.

Goodfellow & Steven is a quality baker, if less sophisticated than Fisher & Donaldson. All the same, its buns and pies have delighted generations. Their popular Celebration Cakes service provides tasty cakes for birthdays and other special occasions and you can count on them to come up with themed cakes to cover everything from Halloween to St Andrew's Day. They also sell sandwiches, hot pies and bridies to take away.

WALLACE'S, LAND O' CAKES
8 Crichton Street; Dura Street

Sadly, only two small shops remain of the Wallace empire, although their success at the World Pie Championships for 2002 looks to be leading them into expansion. Wallace's managed to scoop no less than three top prizes for their pies and bridies, and were named

'Savoury Baker of the Year'. They've always been famous for their pies (or 'pehs', as they're known in Dundee) and bridies, which come in plain ('plehn') or onion ('ingin') varieties. Few of you will be unfamiliar with the Dundonian pie-shop ditty:

> 'Geez ane o' they pehs, an' twa bridies'
> 'Plehn anes or ingin anes?'
> 'Eh, eh'll hae a plehn ane, an' an ingin ane an' a'.'

It's really not that hard to say, but many a non-Dundonian has tried and failed to successfully recite this.

Wallace's are a long-standing popular bakers who are trusty suppliers of the more traditional fare – pies, sausage rolls, tattie scones, yum yums, and I'm sure they used to make 'sair heids', a small iced sponge cake with a bandage round it. Their range of pies is vast: in addition to the traditional meat one, you can also buy bean, macaroni or mince ones, to name but a few.

Coffee and Tea

BRAITHWAITE'S
6 Castle Street

One of the finest and best-loved of Dundee's shops, and a personal favourite. Braithwaite's have been supplying the good people of Dundee with excellent tea and coffee since around 1900, although they didn't move to their present address until 1932. The original shop, in the old Pillars building in Crichton Street, actually opened its aromatic doors in 1868, but was then in the hands of a James Steel, who handed over his caffeine crown to his nephew, which was when it became Braithwaite's. So, it's essentially been in the family since it first opened 134 years ago.

It has a remarkable interior and as most of the original fittings were moved from one shop to the other (including the door) its Victorian splendour is thoroughly intact. Behind the counter (one of the few things to have been replaced, purely due to it being worn out), loose tea is kept in the gorgeous tea bins, with their peeling lacquer and engraved wooden lids. Above, the carved shelving unit has seen a lot of action, with over a century's worth of jars and tins being slid off its shelves. Also original are the stately brass scales, although the weights had to be replaced when it became illegal to sell non-metric measures. There's no point in being a historical gem if you can't come up with the goods and so, not surprisingly, everything on sale is of top quality. Spoilt for choice, their coffees include Kenya AA, Costa Rica, and Papua New Guinea Organic; teas on offer include the traditional Darjeeling and Assam, and the more unusual Gunpowder and Formosa Oolong.

The Mr Braithwaite currently in residence is a fount of knowledge, and will happily enter into discussion, whether it be to answer queries you may have about the massive variety of coffee-making devices, or a discourse on the coffee plantations of Guatemala. You can also buy local produce such as marmalade and honey in jars and on the comb, some of the honey being Braithwaite's own.

You can spot a Braithwaite's shopper from 30 paces by the aroma creeping out of their shopping bag.

Around the World

CHINESE SUPERMARKET
(Matthew's Foods)
Gellatly Street

This is a recent and very welcome addition to the Dundee shopping experience, suitable for the individual as well as the catering world.

They sell a whole bunch of stuff, from the familiar to the exotic and the bizarre. The first product I saw on entering was vacuum-packed jellyfish; this set a precedent for what was to come. A good fruit-and-veg section includes fresh water-chestnuts, papayas, fresh arrowroot, banana leaves and hairy melons (yes, that's really what they're called). You can also buy more familiar vegetables – carrots, garlic, etc. As well as fresh bananas you can also buy whole tinned ones, which was a first for me.

There's a whole aisle dedicated to the countless members of the noodle world, and sealed bags of shredded squid and Tasty Roasted Fish. If you're feeling adventurous, or foolhardy, have a peek in the freezer section. There you'll find blanched squid, lotus root, an abundance of frozen fish (including red snapper and ribbon fish) and a selection of frozen pig parts, such as uterus and spleen. If that's all too much, you could always plump for the peas. Heading back down the aisles you'll find sheets of dried bean curd, tins of pickled lettuce, large bags of dried mushrooms, an 'Instant Chrysanthemum Drink', and a whole host of different soy sauces. If you're planning a dinner party, you'd be a fool not to stock up with an 11 lb bag of chilli powder for £7.50.

After all this, I went home with a couple of peppers, an aubergine and some black-bean sauce. Pathetic.

CONTINENTAL SHOP
146 Hilltown
(There's no shop sign at present. This is a couple of doors down from the Hilltown Post Office.)

Halfway up the steep and hilly Hilltown lies my favourite Asian grocers. They're brilliant for stocking up on basics such as spices, lentils and rice, and are among the cheapest in town. If you enjoy experimenting with food, you'll have a ball here. The fridge is full of gorgeous-looking Indian sweet cakes, paneer cheese and Mrs Unis' onion bhajees, not forgetting the Fresh Excellent Dates. They sell many things I'd never heard of, such as puck cream and fragrant wood slice. If you're into making your own Indian breads, look no further for gram and chapatti flour. There's an interesting selection of vegetables, most of which I couldn't identify, but I did recognise baby aubergines and fresh coriander. They also supply halal meat and chicken. It's easy to be overcome with indecision when faced with the huge choice of curry pastes and pickles on the shelves, and their range of Indian snacks puts the ubiquitous Bombay mix well in the shade. A particular favourite is 'Chin Chin', which really is sublime, with its overtones of garlic and cashew nuts aplenty. Other delights include various packs of olives, including some with paprika and garlic; jars of vine leaves; tins of straw mushrooms and a plethora of chilli sauces.

They used to rent out Bollywood videos, but I haven't spotted any for a while. However, DCA always show one or two of these movies a month if you're suffering withdrawal symptoms.

Fish

McLEISH'S
Castle Street
Brook Street, Broughty Ferry

Another Dundee stalwart, McLeish's is renowned for its quality fish and seafood. I have it on good authority that they're probably the best in town. Apparently, their Arbroath smokie pâté is an absolute winner. Depending on the day of the week, you can choose from whole rainbow trout, filleted sea bass, fresh squid, peppered mackerel, crab and monkfish – also whole, filleted or steaks of salmon, to name but a few.

McLeish's also has a deli counter, with a huge selection of all things meaty, from the humble pie to a choice of three kinds of Polish sausage, including Wiejska. There's also a large range of cold meats, from corned beef to jellied veal. Their own potato fritters, vegetable pakoras, samosas and pre-cooked Indian meals are extremely tasty and popular. One of my recommendations for a homespun lunch is the Pakora Piece; McLeish's pakora wedged inside one of their fine crusty rolls. The addition of something moist helps – I recommend their home-made creamy coleslaw, or alfalfa sprouts from Tayhealth round the corner. A hot food take-away counter here offers proper baked tatties with a variety of their own delicacies (mostly meat); mince or sausages with mashed tatties; home-made soup, and the increasingly popular wrap (puff pastry rather than Puff Daddy). The staff here are always cheery and helpful, however busy, and I reckon are some of the best in town.

Healthy/Organic

TAYHEALTH
42–44 Commercial Street

Believe it or not Tayhealth started out life in Albert Street – aye, in the Stobie. I was a regular then, and am proud to say I still am. Taking up residence in its current home in Commercial Street, Sandy Constable has run the only – and therefore the best – health food/wholefood store in Dundee. Sadly, he has now retired and I shall miss our idle, if at times surreal, banter. The shop still remains in the family.

If it's lentils you're after, you're in the right shop, be it green, red, brown, puy or organic; indeed, any grain or pulse your heart desires can be found on their wholesome shelves. Other good things you can buy here include: an assortment of teas and herbal infusions; the delectable Tartex pâté in its many guises; the unsurpassable Green & Black's organic chocolate (if you haven't tried this, now's your chance to become addicted), and a plethora of jars and tubs of honeys, jams and peanut butters.

They also sell one of the most delicious foodstuffs in the world: Engine Shed's organic smoked tofu, which is made in Edinburgh. It truly is the ambrosia of the soya bean world. Also to be found in the fridge are a variety of joke cheeses and meats, along with various bags of sprouts (not Brussels). Tayhealth is the only place in town where you'll find proper, locally produced free-range eggs from happy 'rinnin' aboot' hens.

Around the two counters is an inordinate bank of jars of oil capsules, vitamins and minerals, while some soap and shampoo shies away in the window. The loyal and knowledgeable staff of Tayhealth will gladly help you choose the right shade of lentil, or strength of primrose oil; if you're very lucky, they might even tell you an entertaining story. But I'm not promising.

One-off Supermarket

PRODUCE DIRECT
274 Perth Road

It's a familiar scene – you're flicking through a recipe book and have finally hit on the perfect dish, but there's always one ingredient that either you've never heard of, or is unlikely to have graced Dundee with its presence. Is it dried galangal you're after? Roasted seaweed perhaps? Panic not. This is where Produce Direct come to the rescue. Of course, they have all the usual standards you need, but it's also an Aladdin's cave of more unusual and even exotic delicacies. Everyone is catered for, with gluten-free biscuits, Wicken Fen vegetarian sausages, organic crispbreads and Russian rye bread sitting alongside Sugar Puffs and baked beans. Other interesting produce to grace these aisles includes: tins of stuffed vine leaves, six types of olive oil, dried shitake mushrooms, French lavender marinade, and the tiniest pasta stars you've ever seen. A range of jams, chutneys and the like, prepared especially for Produce Direct, goes under the name 'Fat Bobs'; these treats in jars take the form of raspberry curd, damson preserve, volcanic lime pickle (which looks pretty evil) and Rascal's Relish. Their selection of Indian and Chinese products includes an extensive range of Blue Dragon products, from fortune cookies to minced coriander. It's the first shop I've come across that sells Shin Cup, the Korean equivalent of Pot Noodle. There's a lot more besides, but hopefully this has whetted your appetite enough to give it a whirl. There's a decent deli counter with fresh parmesan, Polish sausage rings, and something called Flat Kassler, which sounds like a movie action hero. Good bread, too.

On top of all this, they have the cheek to have a decent selection of wine and some excellent beers, including Ruddles Organic, Old Speckled Hen, Caledonian 80/- and Budvar.

Produce Direct may be a dwarf in a world full of supermarket giants, but it knows how to stand its ground. All this, and you might even get to swing your basket to the dulcet tones of Suzi Quatro.

GIFTS, CRAFTS AND GALLERY SHOPS

THE APPLE TREE
129 Nethergate

This is the more upmarket neighbour of Rockhaven (see below). The Apple Tree had a bit of a facelift recently and is now a lot more neat and tidy. I kind of liked its slightly haphazard arrangements, with eggcups and wooden clocks sharing shelf space with glove puppets and chess sets. Jewellery now sparkles all around, and if you're looking for moderately priced sophistication you've hit the spot. Individually made pieces rub up against more market-friendly ones, such as the Ola Gorie range. There's also a selection of posh watches and clocks. The Apple Tree is *the* place to buy a Tula leather purse or handbag, although you'll have to shake all the change out of your old purse to be able to afford one.

There's still a large selection of greeting cards through the back, but it's not as selective as it used to be. Some hand-thrown mugs and bowls sit next to the usual array of candles, picture frames and dinky boxes. It's good for unusual Christmas décorations and their wrapping paper is gorgeous. I also spied some very stylish chopsticks. I was very tempted to buy some stunning soap with Scottie dogs on it, but I couldn't justify spending £5.85 on a bar of novelty soap which would never come out of the wrapper.

DCA
Nethergate

Beautiful gifts for beautiful people. DCA's shop is essentially a small selling gallery of work by artists and craftspeople. Much of the work is by Scottish artists, some being graduates from the Art College up the road. There are usually around 30 different artists' works on sale, with a wide range of ceramic work, jewellery, textiles (anything from hand-made ties to felt bowls) and intricate paper sculpture. All are individual pieces, and are priced accordingly. Not for those on a budget, or the financially faint-hearted. A lot of the work is quite gorgeous though, so if you're feeling a bit flush, why not treat yourself to a quality pair of earrings or a cruet set to astound your friends with. On the staircase that leads up to the small gallery above the shop are shelves with a selection of art books, mostly contemporary. There are also arts magazines and journals, and a selective choice of cards and gift wrap.

INDIGO HOUSE
69 Perth Road

A feast for the eyes, this beautiful shop is a very recent and welcome addition to the Dundee shopping scene. Jam-packed with wares from around the world – Thailand, India, Morocco and Vietnam for starters. It's a challenge not to go home with something, whether it's a simple candle decorated with real flowers, a hand-stitched cushion cover or bedspread, or a gorgeous lacquered photograph album. There are some interesting smells too, especially the Thai palm leaf boxes, which have been smoked and smell good enough to eat. There's an abundance of unusual picture frames, silver jewellery, hand-woven rugs – even a belly dancing outfit can be found here. Also, a range of traditional furniture can be ordered, with some pieces on display. The prices are pretty reasonable, and there is a policy to support fair trade suppliers. Run by a very friendly and informative couple, Indigo House is a much-needed outlet in Dundee, and I shall definitely be back. This is the place to come to brighten up your, or someone else's, home.

McGREGORS
2–4 South Tay Street

A newish gift shop, selling some decent greetings cards and wrapping paper. It also sells luxury cushion trays, wooden skipping ropes with interchangeable handles and Mr Men rucksacks. One of the best items they were selling when I was last in was an embroidered fabric Scottish Premier Football League, with all the teams and position numbers fitted with Velcro, so you could move them round with the changing fortunes of the teams. Useful for teaching your three-year-old how soul destroying being a football fan in Dundee can be. That's what I call a real education. They also sell the usual fare of candles, frames, jewellery, and very small books.

ROCKHAVEN
131 Nethergate

Not, as the name suggests, a haven for rocks, but they do deal in beads, some of which could pass as small stones. In fact, most of your crafty requirements can be found here: all things beady, clasps, wire, raffia, stick-on sequins by the yard, bags of sticks, pipe cleaners, and an abundance of glittery threads and embroidery materials. They also have a number of craft kits, including one for a potato clock.

If you don't fancy making your own, you can choose from their selection of inexpensive jewellery that someone else made earlier; much of this has a Scottish flavour, with Celtic designs featuring prominently. They also do an assortment of greetings cards and postcards.

There's a good selection for Miffy fans such as mousemats, pencil tins, notebooks, badges and even a mini Miffy in a bag. There's also a range of Winnie the Pooh, Elmer, Paddington and Purple Ronnie merchandise. They stock rubber snakes and scary spiders too.

WESTPORT GALLERY
3 Old Hawkhill

The Westport Gallery have narrowed down their range of goods over the last couple of years. They used to have a busier selection of wares – what they sell now is similar but there's just less to choose from. Some modernist leather settees take up a fair bit of space now, and the units in the centre of the shop display a limited choice of plates, cups and glasses. Some of it's very reasonably priced, the Proste range is good, and you could put a whole set together pretty cheaply. If this is all a bit sensible for you, you could always splash out on a metal juice carton container for around £28. There's a large amount of glassware and candles, and a stand of Neal's Yard Remedies products. Also, a good selection of unusual and affordable contemporary jewellery, as well as some considerably more pricey antique jewellery and pocket watches. The staff are helpful, if occasionally a little over enthusiastic about your choice of purchase.

Across the road, the sister shop sells jewellery, candles and a range of ethnic-looking furniture, with names like 'Opium Table' (a bit risqué) and 'Occasional Table' (which is far more British, and presumably isn't used as often as the first).

COLLECTABLES

ALASTAIR JAMIESON
212 Perth Road
Tel: 01382 322017

I first came across the curious world of Alastair Jamieson (herein referred to as AJ) when he had a shop above Alan Beaton Interiors. I spent months coveting a tartan picnic set, which, by the time I decided to actually buy it, was gone. When he moved to his present address, I vowed never to let such an opportunity pass me by again. Needless to say, my house is now full of nonsense. Good nonsense, of course.

What AJ sells are best described as 'collectables', although this doesn't do justice to the bizarre world he occupies. If you're after a 1978 *Blue Peter* annual, an original edition of *Mastermind*, a 1960s standard lamp, or an old jukebox, it's unlikely you won't have been here before. If you haven't, you're in for a treat. Whether you like to reminisce over those old annuals and toys you once had, but that your mum chucked out while your back was turned, or you genuinely want to brighten your home with a piece of furniture the neighbours definitely *won't* have, a visit to AJ's will cheer up your day.

The collectables are mostly from the '50s, '60s and '70s, although some date further back. These may include, for example: Princess Margaret's wedding book, a 1950s chest expander ('For Physical Perfection' – which was 24 shillings, but is now £4.99), a *Van der Valk* annual, Bakelite ware, jelly moulds, a 1970 Diddymen mug, a skating bartender (which has to be seen to be believed), various badges and tin toys. Some of the more unusual items to have appeared include: a collection of antique condoms and dutch caps from the 1930s bearing the name 'LamButt' (ooh, er, missus . . .) and a nasal douche from the late 1800s which AJ eloquently describes as 'a hideous antique nose enema'. Lovely. He recently sold (on the internet) an annoying phone call from his wife's cousin. This had the starting price of 1p and eventually went for £10.01. I believe she's now something of a celebrity. His latest star is a cock castration kit. Go see for yourself.

BIG BAIRN
Westport
See 'Books (Not so New)' section.

CORNUCOPIA
15 King Street
Tel: 01382 224946

This is a teeny weeny shop, which you may have walked past many times and not even noticed. It's at the bottom end of King Street, not far from the front of the Wellgate, just a bit further up than the Town House. It's a basement premises though, so it's easy to miss. What it mostly sells are collectables, in the form of stamps, coins, military medals and bank-notes. There are also some old postcards, including some great ones of old Dundee, with some unusual ones of Dundee personalities. A lovely set of Snow White and the Seven Dwarfs postcards was displayed in the hall, which seemed quite apt, given how tiny the shop is. There's a small cabinet (of course) of Dinky and Corgi toys. The one that caught my eye was a model of Dick Dastardly and his dog Mutley in their flying machine. Wonderful.

ART MATERIALS AND STATIONERS

BURNS AND HARRIS
97–99 Commercial Street

Unfortunately for the artists of Dundee, there is only one art shop assigned to their needs. There is an excellent one situated in the Art College, but it isn't open to the general public, more's the pity. It's not that Burns and Harris (herein known as B&H) is bad, it's just not particularly good. They stock all the basic requirements, such as paint (always a good start for an art shop), oil, acrylic and watercolours of varying qualities. There's also a selection of brushes, sketch pads, inks, colouring pencils, oil and chalk pastels, and a very wide range of plastic paint palettes. They're pretty pricey though, with your average sheet of watercolour paper setting you back around £7. No room for mistakes, then. For a city with an art college and a large community of working artists, it would do B&H no harm to have a bit of competition. Not all the staff seem to have a specialist knowledge in art materials, so it's best to do your homework before embarking on a shopping spree.

They're also a stationers and have the usual packed shelves of sticking devices, writing implements and, most notably, they are the only place in town to stock proper policemen's notebooks and old-fashioned autograph books.

Airfix kits also feature (the Westland Gazelle caught my eye), with a large range of Humbrol enamel paints to match. There are also numerous jigsaws and games, including Mah Jong and Ludo. There's proof here that painting-by-numbers is as popular as ever, as is building famous landmarks from matchsticks (bags of 5,000 available). If you're getting married, B&H can organise that too – not the whole thing, just your stationery.

At Christmas time, B&H sell an extraordinary amount of seasonal tack. Amongst the past offerings were a musical rocking Santa figure, an interactive snowman, fibre-optic trees and a variety of distinctly inartistic lighting displays. Although they do a good line in kitsch Scottish calendars, so they are redeemed.

SCOTTISH

SUTHERLANDS
90 Nethergate

One of my favourite shops to browse in, Sutherlands is the archetypal Scottish shop, with an extraordinary range of quality, from the totally shabby, to the very fine indeed. One of my finest purchases here was a wee furry Scottie dog with a tartan tammy which, when pressed, plays 'Scotland the Brave'. Now there's class for you. They also sell musical cards along the same lines. I was touched to see that Sutherlands continue to sell the stuff I used to buy my gran and grandad for Christmas: plastic back scratchers with full-cheeked pipers on them, and those wee circular metal desk calendars – featuring, presumably, the piper's cousin. For children, you can choose from a pair of furry Loch Ness Monster booties, a Scottie dog bib, and various tartan frocks. An excess of badly modelled figures of golfers and dogs appear alongside some excellent coasters and table mats.

On the classier side, you can purchase a Glengarry here (as an alternative to the 'See You Jimmy' hat) – also ties, bow ties, scarves, stoles and travelling rugs in any number of tartans. There's also a good range of sporrans, kilt pins, and a selection of quaichs (a traditional drinking bowl for the partaking of a wee dram). A revolving case displays a large amount of Scottish jewellery, mostly featuring thistles.

BOOKSHOPS (New)

JAMES THIN
7–8 High Street
Tel: 01382 223999

The first of two proper bookshops to set up camp in Dundee, and not before time. We only had John Menzies before this, so this was a welcome arrival. Thin's don't have an incredible selection of books, but they support local publications, have a good Scottish selection, and are Dundee's main stockist of Mills & Boon.

Also a stationers, they have the usual array of rubber bands, crêpe paper and photo albums downstairs, along with all manner of pens and pencils. They used to stock a well-chosen selection of greeting cards, but the arrival of W.H. Smith has caused an expansion and dumbing down in this department. Thin's also sell a large range of jigsaws (my current favourite being one of some Brussels sprouts) and a selection of board games. They also now stock videos.

WATERSTONE'S
35 Commercial Street
Tel: 01382 200322

This is by far the best bookshop in town. Despite a slightly contentious facelift (some love it, others don't), they still stock an incredible range of books, displayed in a browser-friendly fashion. The staff are knowledgeable and very helpful.

Whether you want to make your own film, learn the rules of badminton, find out what goes on in the head of the Clangers' creator, learn how to make the perfect scone, or read about a mouse whose dream is to become a famous balalaika player, you'll find it all here. If you can't, they'll order it. Waterstone's also stock a good range of maps, greeting cards and wrapping paper.

A fairly recent addition here is a Costa café in the upstairs balcony space, where they used to keep the prams in the Toymaster days. This is the most pleasant of Dundee's three Costas, with a relaxed atmosphere – the perfect place to rest your weary shopping bones.

BOOKS (Not so new)

BIG BAIRN
16a Westport
Tel: 01382 220225

Annuals played a big part in my life when I was a lass. Every Christmas morning, I would wake to find one on the end of my bed. This was a cunning ploy by my parents to keep my siblings and I in bed for an extra hour, and it worked. This tiny wee bookshop is stuffed to the gunnels with childhood memories. If only my mum hadn't thrown out all those *Bunty* annuals . . . Children's annuals of all kinds can be found here, with an entire bookcase devoted to *The Beano*, *The Dandy*, *Oor Wullie* and *The Broons*. There's also a small section of old edition comics, mostly from the '70s. More unusual annuals you might find here range from *Daktari* to *Dr Kildare* (a cartoon version of the 'popular television series' – this must have been a one-off, surely?). There's also an abundance of *Victor* and *Dr Who*. It's not just about annuals, though. This very well-ordered shop specialises in rare, out-of-print, first edition, antiquarian, and sometimes just plain *old* books on many subjects. As well as a good range of hardback fiction titles, you'll find sections on Art, Cookery, Biography, and Nature, amongst others. There's a fine selection of children's books too. It's quite a nostalgia trip coming in here, and I had a good laugh leafing through some TV related 'novels', including *Sapphire and Steel*, and *Starsky and Hutch*. They buy as well as sell, and if they don't have what you're looking for, they'll try to find it for you. The owner is friendly and very helpful, but will happily leave you alone to browse. If you become a regular, the 'New This Week' section will keep you up to date with the latest acquisitions, and there's even a wee cabinet of collectables to give your eyes a rest from squinting sideways at the books.

IRONMONGERS

DAVID BOTTOM
2 Peter Street
Tel: 01382 227750

The great thing about Bottom's is that whether you're buying an icing nozzle or a claw hammer, you know you're going to get the best quality. Maybe you can get stuff cheaper up in B&Q or some other DIY superstore, but you can't buy the expertise or personal touch that you're guaranteed to get from this well-run family business. Like the Duracell bunny, a fish slice from here will outlast your average one in the haddock-flipping arena. Suppliers of hardware and kitchen/domestic ware, you can buy anything from a single screw to a full tool-kit, or a doormat to a paella pan. Other handy things they sell include stepladders, rolling pins, pulley cord, aprons, baking tins, clothes dryers, wood stain, lengths of chain, bath plugs, saws – and the best quality kitchen utensils and saucepans you could

wish for. Bottom's carry unusual ranges, some of which you won't find anywhere else in Dundee. So the next time you're coming out of Marks and Spencer or Tesco metro, pop in for a wee nosey. It'll save you a couple of bus fares, and the lovely people who work here will be able to advise you on the best thing to use for anything.

NEWSAGENTS

Dundee is full of newsagents. They appear on virtually every street corner, but there are one or two in the city centre which keep more unusual titles and they deserve a mention.

CITY NEWSAGENTS
Nethergate/Perth Road

Until recently, this was the only outlet for *The List* magazine. They also stock specialist titles such as *Linedancer* and *Truckers*. It's a pleasant change to see the top shelf as an absolutely porn-free zone. Run by a very friendly man who also does a good line in sweeties.

NETHERGATE NEWS
78 Nethergate

This shop has an incredible selection of magazines. Everything from *The Literary Review* to *Model Helicopter World, Coin News, Scottish Curler*, and an abundance of publications on trout, wrestling and hairstyles. Unfortunately, they are also serious purveyors of porn, with everything from *Escort* to *Lesbian Sex Fest*.

Grocery goods include biscuits and tights.

RECORD SHOPS – Second-Hand

GROUCHO'S
132 Nethergate
Tel: 01382 228496

Groucho's is a Dundee institution. It started out life on the Perth Road in 1976, then moved to the Marketgait, next to the now demolished Angus Hotel. It then had a temporary home in the old Overgate (one of the few decent shops there), finally coming to rest at its present address in the Nethergate. Run by a man named Breeks (no other known name), Groucho's is an emporium of second-hand music. It's now mostly CDs, but there's still a good selection of vinyl, tapes, and 7-inch singles. You'll find everything here, from Lulu to Limp Bizkit, The Tremeloes to Tricky, and Jimmy Osmond to Jimi Hendrix.

Groucho's is the place to come should you wish to sell or exchange your unwanted records. There are many nostalgic '60s and '70s singles at very good prices – if your original copy of David Cassidy's 'How Can I Be Sure' is just too scratched to play any more, the chances are you'll be able to replace it here. I believe, though, he refuses to stock anything by the Bay City Rollers, to the point that they have a special box where anything by the BCRs is duly smashed to smithereens. Fair enough. There are also loads of classic singles, such as Frank Sinatra, etc. There's an abundance of 'cheapo' vinyl for £1 and under; you might find some treasures if you have time to delve into Groucho's musty past. They came up trumps for me just the other day. I had my entire vinyl collection stolen many years ago and the one album I could never replace was the most cherished one – my first ever LP, the *Artistocats* soundtrack, which I'd had since I was about six years old. Lo and behold, the exact same record, with the original gatefold sleeve complete with story book, was lurking among the cheapo section, and was promptly bought by me. One very happy customer.

You'll find a few new CDs here, from the likes of local men Michael Marra and Saint Andrew, which are hard to find elsewhere in town. There's also a selection of second-hand videos and various comics and magazines, such as *Viz* and the *Freak Brothers*. Groucho's is also a booking centre for gigs in Dundee, as well as out of town, often with organised transport.

With the opening in town of a branch of the very fine budget boys Fopp, a number of people voiced worries about the competition, but I'm pleased to say that Groucho's seems as busy as ever. There'll always be something here that you can't get elsewhere, and probably cheaper. And in case you didn't know, breeks is Scottish for trousers.

JOKE SHOPS AND FANCY DRESS

Dundee, sadly, hasn't any really brilliant joke shops, such as Tam Shepherd's in Glasgow, or U Need Us in Portsmouth (a long way to go, I know, but it sells everything). When I was a kid, there was a place in the Seagate, if my memory isn't fooling me, which I frequented most Saturdays. However, you can buy the basic stuff, such as bloody fingers, whoopee cushions, joke jobbies, and six-way moustaches at the following places.

CUNNINGHAM'S
10 St Andrews Street

Cunningham's also sell an amount of fancy-dress gear: policemen's helmets, elves' ears, that sort of thing. There's a reasonable selection of moustaches too. I'm pleased to see they've ditched the porn mags.

PARTY ANIMALS
Lochee High Street

More party than joke.

MASQUERADE
152 Strathmartine Road
Tel: 01382 810660

Fancy dress rather than joke.

A FEW SHOPPING EXTRAS

CITY QUAY FACTORY OUTLET
Camperdown Street
(Down at the docks, this side of the Unicorn)

There's not much to say about this, other than it is in a beautiful location, but sadly it doesn't inspire me to go shopping here. It's a range of factory outlet shops selling clothes, books, nuts, toys and bed linen. The Oasis café claims to offer 'modern British meals with tastes from around the world', but the most exotic dishes I could find on their menu were savoury mince, stovies and macaroni cheese. One of the big draws was to be the opening of a large Harry Ramsden's fish-and-chip shop, but this now looks unlikely to materialise. If you find yourself down this way, enjoy the view and have a nosey on board the *Unicorn*.

DUNDEE FARMERS' MARKET
Shore Terrace
Tel: 01382 434067 for information

Once a month, between May and October, Shore Terrace is taken over by the local farmers, selling their own produce. There's locally farmed ostrich meat, free-range eggs, vegetables, fish, and most other farmable products, including some organic.

DENS ROAD MARKET
39 Dens Road

This was once *the* place to pick up a bargain. Rumour has it that someone once found a Delacroix print here. On the downside, an artist friend once found one of his own prints on sale here for a couple of quid. (I think he bought it back for the frame.) It's basically a second-hand market with stalls selling clothes, antiques, furniture, books, records, and general knick-knacks. There are also some food stalls (which obviously aren't second-hand). In recent years, it's become less interesting, and all looks a bit more organised, with most dealers now wiser to how much folk are willing to pay. No longer can you pick up interesting old plates for 20p, but it's definitely still worth a visit. If you don't find anything, you could always have a game of bingo, or play in the amusement arcade. It's open Tuesdays, Fridays, Saturdays and Sundays, and calls itself 'Dundee's Petticoat Lane'.

ALBERT STREET

I've long been fascinated by the selection of shops in this relatively short stretch of road. There are a phenomenal amount of certain types of shop; here are some statistics.

Bakers: 5
Hairdressers/barbers: 12
Second-hand shops: 6
Second-hand furniture/electrical: 5

Twelve hairdressers – astonishing – although two of these are admittedly in little side streets just off Albert Street, and one is actually a pet's grooming parlour, so you and Rusty can book your bouffants at the same time. There's also a good selection of bakers; one of these has a café attached, where you can buy stovies on a roll. I like the sign in one of the butcher's windows which was advertising the Scotch Pie Club with the slogan, 'Say aye tae a pie'. It's good to see old-established places still flourishing, such as Burnett's Pet Store, and Behrs shoe shop (this used to be *the* place to buy monkey boots). The post office up at the top of the street sells a number of things, such as stamps, Eddie Stobart truck sets, and dominoes in a briefcase. They also have a pinboard in the window with adverts for used prams and cars for sale, and offers to paint you and your pets for Christmas. Further down, as Albert Street becomes Princes Street, the sight of Vince Chalmers Guitar Centre almost brought a tear to my eye. It brought back memories of going there for guitar lessons as a 15 year old. I never got beyond a simplified version of The Shadows' 'Apache'. If only he'd taught me 'Stairway to Heaven', I might be a world-class guitarist now.

LOCHEE HIGH STREET

There's something about the name 'Lochee' that just couldn't belong anywhere other than Dundee. The folk of Lochee are really well catered for; the High Street itself provides enough for a small town. It's not quite in the same league as Albert Street for hairdressers, but their statistics are quite impressive for a single street.

Banks: 4
Bakers: 4
Cafés: 3
Hairdressers/barbers: 4
Pubs: 6
Second-hand shops: 3

There are also shoe shops, butchers, three flower shops and a fishing-tackle shop, plus a couple of fish shops just in case you don't catch anything. If it's a joke biscuit or moustache you're after, Party Animals is the place for you. All this, and a Woolworths and Fisher & Donaldson into the bargain. What more could you ask for?

Well, if you do need anything else, Lochee has its own Tesco store in the Stack Leisure Park, the former Camperdown Works. It's about the only thing left in a leisure park that's so leisurely, it's come to a standstill. It's too boring to list all the things that have closed down, as they weren't that interesting to begin with, but what does remain, apart from Tesco, is the Megabowl, with a pool hall attached, and I think the bingo may still be going. Mind you, they've got the Rialto to contend with, so its days may be numbered.

Buses to Lochee from City Centre: 17, 28, 29.

5

Where to Walk: Walks In and Around Dundee

SEED SHOWERS AND LOST LIGHTHOUSES – A SHORT WALK AROUND THE ARTISTIC, ARCHITECTURAL AND THE CURIOUS, ON THE STREETS OF DUNDEE.

Firstly, I must emphasise that this is not a history lesson, nor is it a definitive tour of all the picturesque views in the city, nor even an account of the most significant pieces of public art on Dundee's fair streets. Instead, this is but a short walk through the city and a thoughtful conversation about the sights you may stumble upon along the way. Some of the discussion has been read and remembered (from somewhere or other), some has been overheard (mostly reliable hearsay), and some is just observed – a mixture of fact and informed street banter. As with most walks we will not notice (and therefore make comment about) everything, but hopefully we will take our time and notice more than we usually do whilst strolling about the city.

To make the best use of this text you should: get out of your armchair – look out of the window and check that it is a sunny day – put on some comfortable walking shoes – put *The Dundee Handbook* in your pocket – and make your way to the Mercat Cross on the Nethergate. On reaching the Cross you should open the book and follow the journey. It should take about two hours at a steady pace (feel free to take along a walking companion as an extra pair of inquisitive eyes).

Okay, if you're ready, we will begin . . .

We start in Dundee city centre, on the **Nethergate**, at the Mercat Cross. This is not the Cross's original position – it has been moving west along the High Street from its first location at the Seagate Tollbooth (erected in the mid-thirteenth century) since the early fifteenth century. The shaft is original, carved in 1586, but the unicorn is a modern copy of the original by Scott Sutherland RSA. It was given its current position in 2000 when the new pedestrian landscaping was completed. This is a good position to start the walk in that it provides an interesting cross section (excuse the pun) of Dundee's architectural diversity.

Immediately to the north of the Cross are the City Churches (St Mary's Church, Mary Slessor Centre and Old Steeple). This is in fact four churches that sit as one – a typical piece of Dundonian economic town planning – that is easily the largest non-cathedral church in Scotland. The Old Steeple (the square tower immediately in front of us) is also the largest, and the best preserved, medieval parish kirk in Scotland. Constructed from various coloured sandstone, we can see that it is divided into two sections by a pinnacled parapet – the main tower below and the belfry above. The great western window above the door is a replacement by Sir Gilbert Scott – a number of years ago I stumbled upon the original medieval tracery stones in a flower bed, under an overhanging tree, in Balgay Park (the stones are still there).

Behind and to the left of the Old Steeple is the new Overgate Centre, opened in March 2000. This 'new shopping experience' replaces the 1963 brutal concrete version that originally destroyed much of Dundee's surviving seventeenth-century heritage in the days before conservation was taken seriously. As shopping malls go this design is unusual in that it is enclosed but single-sided. I'm told that it is possibly the longest two-storey continuously glazed mall in Europe. Once, as I was viewing the Dundee skyline, when I happened to be standing on top of Tayside House (as you do), its dipping, curved, grey roof looked very much like part of a huge Scalextric track that had been set up in the High Street by a big City Council schoolboy. Ironically, the sculptures that we see high in the wall niches of the Overgate seem to have been randomly stuck onto the building by a similar giant hand, like huge décorative brooches. The sculptures (by artist David Wilson) are based around the various activities that used to take place in the original streets of the old Overgate. However, due to their abstraction, placement, and sheer number (all 28 of them), they become little more than curious 'shop sign' emblems that have sadly forgotten their reason to advertise.

If we now continue to turn left, casting our eyes across the Perth Road end of the Nethergate, then continue our gaze left across the road to Meadowside St Paul's with its Gothic Revival façade and tall spire (1850), we see the Mecca tower next door. The building that is now the Mecca Bingo was originally Green's Playhouse, a cinema designed in 1936. For many years the tower was enveloped in a grey metal ribbed shell to supposedly make the façade more up to date. Fortunately, in the late 1990s, the original U-shaped advertising tower, designed by Joseph Emberton as an extravagant Blackpool-type illumination, was restored to its original glory. In the evening the flickering glass panels that randomly go on and off seem charmingly naïve, compared to the surrounding illuminated shop fronts.

So there we are, we haven't moved from the spot yet and we have already seen a thirteenth-century market cross, a fifteenth-century steeple, a nineteenth-century church, a twentieth-century cinema and a twenty-first-century shopping centre – blimey.

Okay, let's go across the road to the Mecca entrance, where many years ago the hooves of Champion the Wonder Horse stood – one of Green's many publicity stunts I believe. Trotting along the street to our right until we are directly in front of Meadowside St Paul's, we find two modest mosaics, by artist Elizabeth McFall (1991). Each sits as a tessellated doormat to the entrances of the church on either side: one in blue/green and one in red/brown.

We now continue towards the **Marketgait** ringroad that cuts the Nethergate in half. If we stop on the corner and look diagonally across the busy traffic to the imposing Royal Bank of Scotland building, we may be able to see a large stained-glass artwork (by artist Liz Rowley) in the glazed southern elevation. To be fair, however, this descending water-twist of glass is best experienced when it is backlit at night (maybe you could come back later when you're out for a pint).

Now turn left along the side of Meadowside St Paul's and past the **Nethergate Underpass** (on the right) designed by Brian Snell and John Gray as part of the same streetscape refurbishment as the previous two mosaics. Now on our left we see *Wave Wall*, another artwork by David Wilson (1986). This is a thoughtfully integrated sculpture that acts as a screen to the small patch of grass between the back of the church hall and the bingo. Its undulating form, stratified stone construction and 'fossil' carvings, make obvious references to this site which lies on the edge of the reclaimed river front. It is also one of those pieces of work that is able to make an immediate visual impact to speeding motorists, but equally, it can engage an inquisitive pedestrian who decides to stop and inspect it more closely.

Another artwork for the passing motorist can be seen immediately across the Marketgait to the south of the *Wave Wall*. *Strange Attractor II*, by artist Alastair White, is a stainless-steel kinetic sculpture made in 1994 as one of two artworks commissioned to celebrate the centenary of Duncan of Jordanstone College of Art (now part of Dundee University). The two spinning triangular steel sails mounted on an independent pendulum counterweight, bear reference to Dundee's spirit of engineering and shipbuilding. Tucked beside this busy bypass, wind gusts blown up from the Tay can either allow *Strange Attractor II* to gently wave at passing traffic or whirl menacingly like a dervish.

Next we cross the Marketgait (at the crossing immediately in front of us) and walk west down into the **Greenmarket**. Here we find ourselves walking across what used to be the old railway yards, and before that the foreshore to the western end of the docks. Now the criss-cross sea of rail tracks has been replaced by a tidy tarmac savannah of car parks that lead us to the Sensation Science Centre (in front) and Dundee Contemporary Arts (on the right). In front of the two buildings we see a tall black steel-and-glass shaft by the roadside. This is an artwork called *Seed Chamber* by artist Alexander Hamilton. As we inspect closer we see that the three sides of the column present photographic showers of drifting seeds, which are beautifully illuminated at night. This vertical display case makes a thoughtful visual connection between the diverse activities that occur in both the Science Centre and the Art Centre opposite. We now turn to the north and make our way to the left side of the Dundee Contemporary Arts building. Opened in March 1999 (Richard Murphy Architects), the new building emerges from the eroded shell of the former brick warehouse of McLeans Garage, slipping past the old structure in a series of copper, glass and steel planes. It's not the first time that art has been installed on this site – in its previous incarnation as a derelict skateboarders' warehouse, many a young creative hand sprayed their 'tags' on the walls. At the steel gate (next to the blue sign) there is a path that will lead us up to the Queen's Hotel and onto the **Perth Road/Nethergate** and the Art Centre's front entrance, two storeys above.

At the top directly across the road from us is Morgan Tower, built in 1794. Constructed as a sturdy block of mansion flats with a bow tower, it is a distinctive landmark on the street that should really have its original harling restored. Rumour has it that with its Venetian windows, ogee roof and Muslim moon weathervane, it was originally commissioned by a well-travelled sea captain by the name of Morgan – possibly a rum-soaked pirate who had hung his swash and buckle up for the last time.

We now cross the road, turn right and then turn left down **South Tay Street** (aligned with the street, the striking glazed entrance into Dundee Contemporary Arts can be seen opposite). The east side of

South Tay Street is probably one of Dundee's best surviving classical terraces (dating from the 1820s), with some good pilastered doorways – look out for number 31, 'Palais de Danse' about halfway down. A short walk along on our left and we come across **Tay Square** and Dundee Rep Theatre. This is an award-winning theatre, built in 1982 by Nicoll Russell Studio, in the form of a bold concrete rectangle whose façade is punctured to reveal the inside to the outside – this is highlighted by the cantilevered staircase leading to the first floor penetrating the front glass wall. In a sense it is a stage within a stage. Unfortunately the development of Tay Square (at a later date) with a guddle of modern piazza furniture (dipping walls, iron railings, light-up paving, benches, mosaics and a 'tree sculpture') does not complement the original focus of the design.

As we continue up South Tay Street we have a very fine view of the 'villas' and green expanses of The Law, rising up to dominate the skyline, with the volcanic apex 'plugged' with the pawn-like war memorial which was erected in 1921.

At the end of the street we reach the **Westport** and the bypass that swept away the old winding streets of Hawkhill. We take a left here and head towards the Globe Bar with its distinctive 1864 clock turret above. Just in front of the Globe we find the 'pyramid toilets' designed by artist Stanley Bonnar – a curious marble-effect floating pyramid with the male and female toilet entrances framed on either side by geometric steel tree canopies. Unfortunately, the floating effect of the pyramid is a little spoilt now with the introduction of a low rail to deter skateboarders and young mountain climbers – pity.

We now continue along the Westport keeping to the left of the Globe, moving up into the northern perimeter of the Dundee University campus. We pass two more pubs (Tally Ho and Mickey Coyle's) and a small car park on our right, until we come to **Hunter Street**. In front of us, perched on a small grass mound, is *The Bridge* by artist Ron Martin. This sculpture, created in Corten steel, with its distinctive ferrous red patina, is based on the bridge of a cello but is reminiscent of one of the many gateways that used to surround the medieval city. To our right there is another good view of The Law but this time you can see a white turreted castle in the middle foreground. This is Dudhope Castle, the remaining two wings of a sixteenth-century palace and hereditary seat of the Scrymgeours, constables of Dundee. In more recent times it has been a woollen mill and a barracks, but has now been converted into business offices. To the left of Hunter Street is Small's Wynd, and if we walked down there we would find ourselves in the university campus with many fine examples of nineteenth- and twentieth-century institutional architecture, with the Geddes Quadrangle (built as a teaching garden in 1909) at its heart.

We, however, will continue up the **Old Hawkhill**, heading west. Unfortunately the only remaining evidence of the old streetscape now is the University Grounds Department warehouse immediately on your right and the cobbles underfoot. Moving along swiftly we pass car parks on either side, the Scandinavian-influenced Belmont halls of residence (1960s) on the left and the grey corrugated block mass of the university sports halls on the right. At the top of the road, we veer to the right along a pedestrian ramp up to the side of the bypass carriageway. To our left is the blue-and-white edifice of the Wellcome Trust Building (1997), the biomedical faculty of the university and a national centre for cancer research. In the large glazed atrium of the north elevation of the building we can see a stained-glass artwork running in two vertical panels through its middle section, by artist Julian Stockes. At closer inspection moving through the atrium staircase the glass work is detailed with beautifully rendered biomedical references – outside it is best experienced at night when the building dominates the skyline like a huge science cathedral. If you do get a chance to go inside, there is also a wall installation behind the reception desk by artist Jake Kempsall, and some rustic furniture by artist Tim Stead at the base of the stairs.

We now cross the **Hawkhill dual carriageway** at the traffic lights to

St Joseph's Primary School and the entrance to **Bellfield Street**. There are a number of artworks along the west side of this street created as part of the Blackness Public Art programme between 1982 and 1985. Firstly, we cross the street to the Whitehall Theatre whose door surround was decorated in mosaic by the Artist Collective in theatrical motifs. A few steps along we find a silkscreen tiled panel set into the wall of Fairfield Garage Services by artist Kenny Munro – this was originally one of four panels depicting old Dundee charabancs, but unfortunately the others have already been lost due to redevelopment. A few steps further, towards the end of the street, are five beautiful (Saltire Award-winning) ceramic panels by artist Keith Donnelly, filling the window embrasures of Alexander Removals red-brick warehouse. When we continue past, if we turn around and look up at the side of the same block, we see a further four ceramic window panels by artist Mike De Haan.

We will shortly be crossing the road and turning down **Blackness Road** to the right, but before we do let's make a quick detour to the front of the concrete façade of the fire station, up to the left. Here we will find an old Shand Mason steam fire engine, with its sparkling brass boiler and gleaming red-and-gold paintwork making it look every bit like the brand new model in a car showroom.

Okay, back down to the corner of Bellfield Street and we'll head east down Blackness Road. This road, on the high ground overlooking the Blackness industrial area, has changed completely since 2000 and the only building left from the densely packed collection of mill buildings and warehouses is the striking vertically proportioned St Joseph's School (1906) on your right. As a minor break in the visual monotony of these new harled living units that have sprung up, we can catch a good view across the Blackness industrial skyline if we stop in the parking drive between house numbers 91–87. This whole area used to be the most densely clustered concentration of mills in Dundee in the mid-1800s. If we look west (to your left) you can see Logie Works and the Coffin Mill – the name of the latter is taken from its shape and also from stories of the grisly deaths of some of its employees (it's haunted, you know). This was Scotland's biggest flax works but has now been converted into flats. In front of us is Burnside Mill (now empty), to the right and further back is Meadow Mill (now artists' studios) and to the right again, Verdant Works (now a Textile Heritage Museum). All were originally involved in the production of jute.

We now continue along Blackness Road until we turn down **Urquhart Street**, on the left. At the bottom of the street is the Royal Oak pub. As we can see by the sign, this hostelry has been here since 1745 when the area was fields and this was one of the main western routes into the city – it's therefore not a bad place to stop and rest your legs and take in some refreshments, if you so wish.

At the Royal Oak we turn right and head east along **Brook Street**. These may not be the most beautiful of streets in Dundee, but their odd collection of garages, warehouses and converted mills and churches give a good indication of the city's honest but changing industrial roots. Brook Street follows the course of the old Scouring Burn Valley, which was the initial water source that supplied the mill industries in the west end (I believe it still runs in a culvert below our feet to this day). We continue to the end of the street, past West Henderson's Wynd and the entrance to the Verdant Works Museum (on the left) and Horsewater Wynd (on the right) and straight on into **Guthrie Street**. A short way down on our right is Blinshall Street. If we look up the street we can see a small chapel-church with a bellcote called St Mary Magdalene, which used to be the central Mission of the largest Episcopal congregation in Scotland. It's now an auction hall, but I'm told that much of its fine wall stencilling still survives under its present whitewashed interior. When we get to the junction of Brown Street we can see the rear façade of Tay Works – continue straight ahead here. Tay Works (1865) was one of the largest textile mills in Britain (650ft long). It has now been converted into university student residences. As we go between the mill buildings at the end of

Guthrie Street and cross the dual carriageway we can look back across the road and see the massive classical splendour of its front elevation stretching the full length of the western side of the **Marketgait** – I believe there used to be a statue of Minerva (Roman goddess of the arts) atop the central pediment.

We are now on the north corner of the junction to the Marketgait and Ward Road. On the quiet turfed corner of this busy street is *Scourin' Burn Burst*, by artist Chris Biddlecombe. This is the second artwork that was commissioned to celebrate the centenary of Duncan of Jordanstone College of Art in 1994 and marks the spot where the Scouring Burn leaves Blackness and enters the city. The natural stone collected from the Sidlaw Hills, the steel tower with its tie rings and 'water gush', and the circular seating with a central release valve, all make references to Dundee's industrial past and allow the installation to sit comfortably in historical ambiguity. Look out for this corner in the springtime when the turf explodes with a riot of floral colour.

We now continue east along **Ward Road**, past the pillared temple front of the Sheriff Court (1860s) for about three minutes until we get to the graveyard on the right and Ward Road becomes **Meadowside**. As the name suggests this area was originally north of the burgh boundary and it was initially Mary Queen of Scots in 1564 who granted this land from the Greyfriars to be a city graveyard. The Howff (or 'meeting place') still remains a quiet refuge in the centre of the busy city, surrounded as it is by high walls and railings. Inside you can stroll along the wonderful closed arcading of the west wall or explore the huge variety of morbid inscriptions on these crumbling monuments to jute barons, seafarers and mill workers. Opposite, on the north side of the street, both buildings support watchful angels that remain vigilant across the traffic – two angels are symbolic of the postal and telegraph services on the old French-inspired post office of 1898 (it's now The Circus nightclub so it's only a matter of time before they trade their modest drapes for a pair of lycra pants); and two of the winged figures are symbolic of literature and justice on the

American-inspired red stone Courier Building of DC Thomson (1902).

We now cross the road to the Courier Building and walk to the end of Meadowside and cross into **Albert Square**. In front of us is the western elevation and renaissance horseshoe staircase of the McManus Galleries (1867), a memorial to Prince Albert, formerly known as the Albert Institute. Before we walk around the outside of the building, however, we are greeted by Robert Burns (1880) in a slightly camp repose across a tree trunk, pen in hand, but missing paper. He seems to be searching for inspiration (surprisingly) from the upper office windows of DC Thomson behind us. Interestingly, these are the same office windows from which, I was once told, a certain cartoonist spied inspiration in the school yard below to create The Bash Street Kids in *The Beano*. The playground is immediately to the right of the Courier Building in front of the impressive neoclassical portico of Dundee High School (1824).

If we continue around the outside of McManus Galleries to the left (clockwise), we are next confronted by George Kinloch (1872) Dundee's first Reform MP, dressed in a gown and appearing to carry what looks remarkably like a spicy wrap of some kind (the Dundonians love their food). Along a little further, in front of the museum entrance, is a fine example of the ubiquitous Queen Victoria in bell-jar frock celebrating her Diamond Jubilee of 1897 (she has obviously had a few too many of George's wraps). If you glance north, across the road, you will also see the elegant façade of the Guardian Royal Exchange, probably Dundee's best 1950s building. Finally, before we cross the road and leave Albert Square at its north-east corner, we meet James Carmichael (1876), an engineer taking a wee breather on one of his old boilers and looking surprisingly like Lurch, the Addams family butler.

On crossing the road we head east down **Panmure Street**. A short distance down on a black concrete wall on our right (just after Caw's), are a series of four stone carvings by artist Gillian Forbes (1998).

These modest reliefs depict various cornucopia shells spilling forth a selection of fruits, vegetables, grains and fish, quietly indicating your entrance into one of Dundee's busiest shopping streets just around the corner. A few steps further down and we turn right into the **Murraygate**. This and the parallel Seagate, to the south, were the original commercial heart of the city and to this day the Murraygate displays Dundee's most eclectic streetscape. It was pedestrianised and re-landscaped in 1992, reinstating the old tramlines with stone paving and new setts and introducing organically styled seating, fencing and bollards by artist David Wilson. If you raise your eyes above the contemporary shop fronts you will see architecture ranging from pink candy modernism, a classical bankers' palazzo, an original Lutyens Marks and Spencer, a 1920s cinema-styled Woolworth building, to a 1911 Arts and Crafts shop front and much more in between – I'll let you explore.

A few steps along the Murraygate on our left is **Peter Street**, a small pend that runs down to the Seagate to the original position of the Mercat Cross. On the ground in the pend we see two funnel-shaped mosaics by artists Chris Kelly and Chris Biddlecombe *(Site Insite)*. The profile of each is taken from the octagonal base of the Mercat Cross – one mosaic filled with water and the other filled with fire. This refers to the rich history of this narrow thoroughfare – as the route through to the Sea Vennel and the site of the Cross Well – and also as the place of witch burning, and Watson's whisky bond fire at the south end and of 'fire and brimstone' sermons by Ranter Johnson in the Independent Methodist Church at the north end. If we now look to our right there is another ground mosaic stretched in front of Tescos, by artist Elizabeth McFall. This simple mosaic utilises a clever tessellated design to describe twisting yarns that refer to Dundee's textile heritage. We now continue down the length of the Murraygate, watching out for all that pick 'n' mix planning, until we reach the junction with **Commercial Street** where we take a left.

We keep to the right-hand side of the street and walk down to the junction with the **Seagate**. At this point, diagonally to our right we see St Paul's Episcopal Cathedral Church perched on the castle rock by Sir George Gilbert Scott in 1853. A fine example of the Gothic Revival, it towers above us at 210ft with a variety of chain-smoking gargoyles guarding its spire. On crossing the road, immediately in front of the cathedral, we meet Admiral Duncan placed on his plinth by artist Janet Scrymgeour Wedderburn in 1997, to mark the bicentenary of the Battle of Camperdown. Unfortunately, the Admiral, who by all accounts was a tall and elegant gentleman, is depicted here looking more like Mr Pickwick about to go in search of some more 'pehs'.

We continue south, down through the ageing grandeur of Commercial Street until we meet **Dock Street** at the bottom. As the name suggests, this used to be the waterfront, with the King William Dock immediately in front of us – if we look down the street to the left we can see what was one of the largest custom houses in Scotland (1843) on the south side of the street in the distance. Now, in front of us, we are confronted with the busy circular access ramp of the Tay Road Bridge (1966) and a curious little park placed in its centre. If we cut diagonally across the small carpark, under the ramp and walk to the south side of the park and look through the trees, we can see a little lost lighthouse in an open park beyond. Sadly, this final remnant of the thriving dock landscape can now only guide the multitude of wild rabbits back into their burrows.

Okay, back across the park, under the Tay Bridge traffic and back onto Dock Street, where we see a thoughtful refurbishment of flats in the centre of the street's north side. Here is a good example of well integrated contemporary art and design placed into an existing historical façade – with modest twisting ironwork by Philip Johnson of Ratho Forge, and a carving focusing on the movement of moon and tides (running along the top) by artist Gillian Forbes. We now cross back over the street and walk to the west until we get to the corner of Castle Street. The large building on the corner (now partly occupied by The Stance and Drum) used to be the Exchange Coffee House.

Designed in 1828 as assembly rooms and a merchant's library, it is another example of the affluence and importance that the shipping industry once had on the city's visual character. We now turn right and walk up **Castle Street**, which was literally blown out of the castle rock using gunpowder in the 1780s. As we move up the street there are two more beautiful examples of Philip Johnson's contemporary wrought ironwork at the gates of Doig Court and Number 36. Alongside these new gates we also find the fine 1919 glazed entrance to the former office of the whisky magnate Sir John Stewart on the right. Further along on the left, above the contemporary shopfronts of Numbers 7–21, we can see the façade of the old Theatre Royal (1825) with a bust of Shakespeare hiding centre-stage, high above, in its pediment.

At the top of Castle Street we enter the pedestrianised **High Street**, the site of the town's old market place – once a rival in size to the Grassmarket in Edinburgh. To our right we can see the triangular pavilion of the Clydesdale Bank (1876) and to the left of that is a bronze sculpture of the Dundee Dragon, designed by artist Alistair Smart and created by artist Tony Morrow. Much loved by the little people of Dundee as a reptile to climb on, its story is part of the city's folklore – evil dragon surreptitiously kills nine maidens and is then subsequently killed by a brave local blacksmith. Ironically I've always thought that the two draped ladies in the ground-floor niches of the Clydesdale Bank could easily double up as a couple of the unfortunate maidens, whilst Britannica, leaning on her trident above, could play the village hero – if the need for such a tableau ever arose.

We now move to the north side of the street and turn to the left. Immediately in front of us at Campbell's Close (Hugh Farquhar's), and also a little further down in Croom's Close, are two more wrought-iron gates by Philip Johnson. Between the two gates, above the shop fronts of Numbers 70–73, is the distressed plaster street front of Gardyne's Land. A historically significant merchant's house, built between the fifteenth and nineteenth centuries, and currently undergoing much-needed restoration by Tayside Building Preservation – it gives a good suggestion of how the old market streetscape would have been. As we continue west down the High Street, just before we come to the junction of **Reform Street**, we overtake Desperate Dan striding back home to the Courier Building, with his dawg and Minnie the Minx mischievously in tow. Another bronze work by artist Tony Morrow, this bizarre Disneyfication of the Scottish comic book acts as another piece of entertainment for those little ladies who like to hang from 6ft cowboys and little boys who like to climb over naughty girls. Curiously, Minnie recently went missing – I was told that she had broken her arm and was in the foundry hospital. But it crossed my mind that she may have gone walkabout (like a holidaying garden gnome) and will possibly turn up firing a broadside of rotten apples at the Admiral, or flicking ink pellets at Rabbie – watch out.

To our left is the colonnaded front of the Caird Hall (1922), acting as a backdrop to the **City Square**, its two fountains designed around the elemental themes of fire, water, air and earth are by artist Lizanne Wood. Across Reform Street junction and in front of Boots is a relief map of the city with three architectural models cast in bronze, by artist Doug Cocker (1995). The models depict the well-known Dundonian landmarks of the Royal Arch (originally beside the King William Dock – now demolished), the Wishart Arch (a relic of the original city walls at the east end of the Seagate) and Cox's Stack (the 280ft Italian-styled chimney of Camperdown Jute Works in Lochee). If we walk diagonally south-west to where the pedestrian area of the High Street stops and we look south down Crichton Street, we see yet another Dundee landmark model. On the right side of the street above the entrance to The Pillars pub is a lovely old model of the Town House (1731) – a building that used to stand on the south side of the High Street, on the site of the present City Square (it was demolished in 1932). The pub gets its name from the ground-level piazza front of the Town House – a meeting place known to locals as 'the Pillars'. Now we continue along the left side of the High Street, past Whitehall

Street and the curious little 'Hickory Dickory' gate beside the jewellers on the left.

We are now in the final stretch of our walk as we proceed west and the **High Street** becomes the **Nethergate** – we can see the Overgate and the City Churches on our right. Before we cross the road and reach the Mercat Cross though, we pass Couttie's Wynd on our left, with a David Wilson bollard at its entrance. This narrow back passage, beside the Trades House pub, is the surviving route (one of two) that ran down to the original dockside in the 1600s. It is interesting to consider the many changes that have washed through the city as we look down this forgotten lane that was once a thriving thoroughfare to the waterfront, and then look across the road to the present throngs of shoppers and workers hovering around the new Overgate.

I hope that this wee walk has opened your eyes to some of the often unnoticed corners of the city and that it may encourage you to look up, down, through and beyond your usual view of these well-trodden streets.

Happy walking (eyes wide open),
Street Dog.

OTHER GREAT WALKS

For serious walking, take the train or bus to Perth and simply head north on the train. Some excellent walking in the Highlands is easily accessed within a daytrip – head for Blairgowrie or Blair Atholl for example.

From Alyth (catch the number 52 bus from the Seagate Bus Station), you can begin the Cataran Trail, a circular 60-mile walk that takes you through the heart of Scotland. A map of the route is available locally (Waterstone's booksellers, Tourist Information). Wooden posts with a heart symbol mark out the trail. If you step up your pace (you will need to cover 30 miles in a day), you could be in Glenshee by the evening, lodging at the tartan spectacle of the Glenshee Hotel (which isn't really very glamorous).

* * *

Take the bus to Elie on the East Neuk of Fife and walk along the Fife Coastal Path toward Dundee. The path follows a beautiful stretch of coastline dotted with old fishing villages. It is easy walking and you could stop off at any one of the villages to jump on a bus back to Dundee. There is an excellent seafood restaurant and bar in St Monan's and a fantastic fish-and-chip shop/restaurant in Anstruther, which clocks up awards on an annual basis, and in August, Pittenweem has a fish festival where you can buy a hot kipper in a bun for your lunch.

Closer to the city, either walk across the Tay Road Bridge (there is a pedestrian walkway), or take a bus to Tayport. Walk down through Tayport towards the River Tay, which at this point is just about to become the North Sea. Stretching south towards Leuchars and St Andrews are Tentsmuir Forest and Sands. Both are glorious. Tentsmuir Forest is great for mountain biking.

IN DUNDEE

Walk up The Law, the highest point in the city. It's a quick walk, and you don't really need a map. Just head in the right direction (north and uphill) and you should find your way. The views are spectacular – over to Perthshire, the Sidlaws and Fife – and you get a great overall view and layout of the city itself.

RECOMMENDED LITERATURE AND MAPS

Dundee City Council have produced a map for Dundee's Green Circular Cycle Route. You don't have to have a bike to take advantage of it – being a footpath too, you can walk, jog, run – anything you feel like doing on foot, basically. Being 26 miles in total, it's ideal if you're planning on becoming a marathon runner. Don't be put off by its mileage – you can come off it at any point. It's currently available from Tourist Information, priced £1.50

There's a good series of wee books on walks, covering areas such as Angus and Dundee (including Angus Glens); East Perthshire (including Perth, Blairgowrie and Dunkeld); South Perthshire (including Crieff, Auchterarder and Kinross), and a number of others. These are called *Hallewell Pocket Walking Guides*. There are approximately 25 walks in each, and they include small maps. Walks are graded for difficulty, and cover short strolls to long hikes. All cost around £2.50.

Ordnance Survey Landranger and Explorer series of maps are always handy if you're feeling a bit adventurous. Available from bookshops and Tourist Information.

6

An A–Z of Odds and Ends

Bandstands

Dundee's bandstand is on Magdalen Green, a charming park beside Magdalen Yard Road. Alarmingly, the council at one time attempted to pull this eighteenth-century icon down; an idiotic notion which was thankfully thwarted by the 'Friends of Magdalen Green Bandstand' group, and it remains fully functional. Every Sunday afternoon during the summer, a changing line-up of brass bands take to the bandstand, entertaining the gathering crowds who seat themselves on the plastic chairs that the council send along in a van. This is great if you want a proper sit-down; I prefer to take a picnic, and spread things out on the grass, with some wine to hand. Sitting here, with the Tay glistening before you, listening to 'The Dambusters' and all your other brassy favourites, is one of the loveliest ways imaginable to while away the sunny Sunday hours.

Bingo

This was once thought of as a pensioner sport, but now it's anyone's game. Many of Dundee's picture houses were turned into bingo halls, but now there's only a few left. The main ones are 'megabingo' halls, run by Mecca. Dundee has two of these, and a handful of others. I have made many sacrifices in the writing of this book, and one of them was to become a member of Mecca Bingo. And all for you.

MECCA BINGO
Playhouse
106–110 Nethergate
Tel: 01382 201580

I imagine the bingo experience is much the same wherever you go, especially if it's in one of the mega halls. Formerly Green's Playhouse, the Mecca has the tiniest, and most unnecessary escalators known to man. They have around six steps on them and are lit up the side, giving them a space-age quality. On the other hand, if you buy an in-house felt-tip pen, they're absolutely huge – I could hardly hold mine in one hand. Given that my friend and I didn't really know the ropes, we were very grateful for the helpful folk on hand to keep us right with our lines across and full houses (not that we got any). There are many things to learn about bingo, but the main ones are – don't sit in someone else's lucky seat; *never* talk during games (unless in very hushed tones) – but do be prepared to have a good laugh. If you're here for the night, macaroni cheese, pies and beer are the cheap-and-cheerful refreshments on offer.

Below are details of some other bingo halls.

GALA BINGO CLUB
Stack Leisure Park
Harefield Road
Lochee
Tel: 01382 400800

MECCA
Douglasfield
Douglas Road
Tel: 01382 508090

RIALTO BINGO CLUB
3 Grays Lane
Lochee
Tel: 01382 611529

Eyes down and all that!

Dundee Dialect

No book about Dundee would be complete without a wee mention of the Dundee accent, world famous for being unfathomable to the untrained ear. There's been an entire book devoted to the subject, Mick McClulskey's very fine (but now out of print) *Dundonian For Beginners*. The accent is difficult to describe, comes in many strengths, and can be hard to get a grip of, but there are many Dundonians who don't speak with *the* Dundee accent. They do, however, use a number of Dundonian words which you will hear from even the most eloquent Dundee mouth. Here are some of my favourite Dundee words and phrases. Spellings are not definitive . . .

'an ingin ane an' a': has already been discussed under 'Pies'
'emphehsehzehs the sehz o' yir ehz': 'emphasises the size of your eyes'
    (Overheard during a discussion on the benefits of blue eyeshadow)
'ekskwisih', is it?': 'exquisite, isn't it?' (On similar subject)
gochels: phlegm, when coughed up or spat out
skek: to look, as in 'gie's a skek at yir *Tully*'
doolies: nose pickings
fleg: fright
let on: to tell, or give the game away
let off: to fart, to expel wind
skiffy: usually used in I-spy (eh speh) games, when you want to be
    given a directional clue. This is given by quickly sliding the palm of
    one hand off the other in the direction of the spied object
choony/chewny: chewing gum

plettie: a kind of platform on each landing of certain tenement
    buildings which aren't fully enclosed
closie: the entrance to a tenement building
cundie: a drain by the side of the road
barkit: very dirty
circle: a traffic roundabout
reedur: a red face as a result of embarrassment
mingin': very, very dirty, to the point of smelling very, very badly
pure mingin': the same, but worse

Football

Despite a huge place in my heart for Dundee United, and a genuine
interest in football, it seemed only right and proper to pass the subject
on to a couple of lifelong supporters and regular attenders of games,
both home and away. It gives me great pleasure, then, to hand you
over now to the two club mascot dogs . . .

FOOTBALL IN DUNDEE

The city of Dundee has a long history of professional football, with a
healthy rivalry between Dundee and Dundee United. Although
football in Scotland is now dominated by the financial might of Celtic
and Rangers, both Dundee teams have proud histories of success at
home and abroad. Amazingly, Dundee is the only city in the UK that
has two teams that have appeared in European Cup semi-finals;
Dundee in 1963, and Dundee United in 1984. Tannadice and Dens
Park are the two closest professional football grounds in the UK,
sharing the same street. Any visitor interested in football should take
a trip up The Law to see just how close Tannadice (United) and Dens
(Dundee) are, separated only by a kiddies' play park.

Until the early '70s, Dundee were undoubtedly the dominant city
club, but following the appointment of Jim McLean as manager in
1972, United enjoyed nearly a quarter of a century of city dominance.

However, United are currently no longer the force they were, and Dundee have had a revival of late. Their respective fortunes are now fairly even, resulting in some of the most exciting derby matches for years. At recent matches between the two, the 'Sold Out' signs have gone up at both grounds.

The Dundee derby gives the city visitor an exciting introduction into the city's football culture, and is highly recommended, especially if combined with visits to some of the fine old pubs that surround both grounds. The Clep is one of Dundee's finest pubs, but also recommended are the Snug, Frew's, Halley's and the Bowbridge. All are listed in the 'Where to Drink' section.

If you want to fit in with the locals at a game, be prepared with the appropriate shout of 'that was closer to going in at Dens/Tannadice' whenever there is a wayward attempt at goal.

There is something about the nature of football culture in Dundee that seems to encourage the strange, the bizarre and the just plain funny. Argentinian World Cup star Claudio Caniggia recently played for Dundee, and he invited Maradona to join him for a one-off match; he never came. An ex-United player won an Oscar for screen-writing rather than diving; Grace Kelly attended Hamish MacAlpine's testimonial match at Tannadice (an event that was immortalised by Michael Marra); and United Chairman Jim McLean physically attacked a BBC reporter during a televised interview. The list is endless.

DUNDEE UNITED – A WEE BIT OF HISTORY

Members of the Irish community in Dundee formed Dundee Hibernian in 1909, the football club that was to become Dundee United. In 1923, after election to the Scottish League, it was decided to drop the 'Hibernian' from the name to widen the potential fan base. The name Dundee City was initially proposed as the new name for the club, but Dundee FC objected to this, and the compromise of 'Dundee United' was reached, although no union had taken place.

United's rise to fame as a force in European football began in the 1960s. A host of Scandinavian imports, including Orjan Persson and Finn Seemann, helped them to reach fifth position in the Scottish League, giving the club a place in the Fairs Cup of 1966–67. During this campaign, United defeated cup holders Barcelona in both legs – a feat which they were to repeat in the 1987 UEFA Cup. The club has the admirable boast that they are the only team in Britain to have beaten Barcelona in every competitive match.

In 1971, Jim McLean, a former Dundee FC player and coach, was appointed as manager of Dundee United, a post in which he was to remain for 22 years. Under his tenure, United were to become one of the new forces in Scottish football, culminating with the League win in the 1982–83 season. This was followed by a place in the UEFA Cup final against Gothenburg in 1986–87. The match, although lost on the pitch, was a triumph for the fans, when they were awarded the Fair Play Award by FIFA, after their extreme graciousness in defeat, applauding the winners off the field. When Jim McLean retired from management in 1993, having won many honours (the Scottish Cup being the only domestic trophy to elude him), he remained with the club as chairman.

The next season, ex-Yugoslav internationalist Ivan Golac (also a former full-back for Southampton, Bournemouth and Manchester City) was appointed as manager. In his first season, Golac led the Tangerines to Scottish Cup victory against Rangers. His training techniques were unconventional to say the least (for example taking the team to look at flowers before the final, rather than talking tactics) but the fans didn't complain, and for a while Golac became an odd hero on Tayside.

Following seasons, however, failed to live up to the initial promise, and United and Golac parted company in March 1995. Then followed a period of upheaval, with a string of managers, including the chairman's younger brother, Tommy McLean, and a mercifully brief sojourn in the First Division. In latter years, United have struggled towards the lower regions of the Premier Division, but are showing signs of improvement under Alex Smith, appointed during the 2000–2001 season. Recently, the old Board was ousted by a group of shareholders (including Jim McLean, who had resigned the chairmanship following the bizarre televised assault mentioned earlier) who have now taken over in a bid to boost the financial fortunes of the club.

Over the past 20 years, United, with their admirable youth policy, have produced many fine players who have found their way into some of the top clubs in the country. Names like Andy Gray, Richard Gough, Ralph Milne, Kevin Gallacher, Billy MacKinlay, Christian Dailly, and Duncan Ferguson all began their careers at Tannadice.

Fans are known as Arabs. The most popular theory for the background to this nickname is set around a harsh winter in 1962–63. Apparently they were so desperate to make the pitch playable, that a tar burner was used to melt the thick snow and ice, and hundreds of tons of sand were spread over it. United seemed to adapt well to this new playing surface, and won 3–0.

A FEW STATISTICS

Ground: Tannadice Park
Capacity: 14,200
Current ticket Price: Adult £16
Address: Tannadice Street, Dundee DD3 7JW
Tel. No.: 01382 833166
Ticketline: 01382 833166
Website: www.dundeeunitedfc.co.uk

Manager: Alex Smith (since season 2000–2001)
Strip: Home – tangerine top, black shorts, tangerine socks
     Away – white top, white shorts, white socks
Top scorer: Peter Mackay – 158 goals in 134 games (1947–54)

Biggest win: 14–0 versus Nithsdale Wanderers, Scottish Cup (1931)
Biggest defeat: 1–12 versus Motherwell, Division Two (1954)

Selected Trophies/Achievements
Scottish League Premier Division Champions 1982–83
Scottish Cup winners 1994; runners-up 1974, '81, '85, '87, '88, and '91
Scottish League Cup winners 1979–80, 1980–81; runners-up 1981–82, 1984–85
UEFA Cup runners-up 1986–87
European Cup semi-finalists 1983–84

Further Reading
Rags to Riches – Mike Watson (David Winter & Son)
Across the Great Divide – Jim Wilkie (Mainstream)

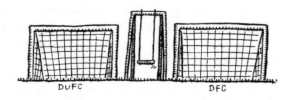

DUFC   DFC

DUNDEE FC – A WEE BIT OF HISTORY

Formed in 1893 by the amalgamation of Our Boys and East End, Dundee have been at their home in Dens Park since 1899. They won the League Cup twice in the 1950s, but it was the early '60s that saw the club with its most talented team to date. Players such as Alex Hamilton, Alan Gilzean, Ian Ure and Gordon Smith were instrumental in DFC winning the League Championship in 1961–62. The following season, they reached the semi-final of the European Cup, defeating Cologne, Sporting Lisbon and Anderlecht, before losing to AC Milan, who went on to lift the trophy.

Since the inception of the Scottish Premier League in 1976, Dundee's inability to hold onto their best players and managers has been reflected in their position in the league, usually struggling for promotion or against relegation. While they had failed to recreate the Cup and League-winning teams of the 1950s and '60s, their greatest rivals, Dundee United, enjoyed unprecedented success. The irony that United prospered during this time is not lost on the Dens Park faithful, given that it was masterminded by a former Dundee player, whom the club had previously rejected as their manager.

That United's success was achieved through an astute youth development and selling policy only highlighted Dundee's need for the club to be properly managed from the boardroom down. In 1997, after 20 years of changing ownership, local brothers Peter and Jimmy Marr took financial control of DFC, which marked the beginning of the current era at Dens Park. They brought in Jocky Scott (a former player for DFC) as manager, and this, combined with the signing of several key players, resulted in them finally winning promotion to the Premier League, having languished in the First Division for four years. The following season, they finished in a more than respectable fifth position, the club's highest placing for 25 years. In 2000, the releasing of Jocky Scott and the appointment of Italian Ivano Bonetti as manager and his brother Dario as assistant, was received with amused scepticism by most commentators on the game.

Although the brothers arrived at Dens with little managerial experience, they both had formidable backgrounds as players in Italy's top clubs. Elder brother Dario had played with Roma, Sampdoria, Milan and Verona; the younger Ivano with Juventus (with Platini), Sampdoria, Bologna and Genoa. When the managers used contacts developed from years of playing in Italy's Serie A to bring in a host of oversees players to the club – including Argentinian legend Claudio Caniggia – not unsurprisingly there was almost universal disbelief. This influx of players, largely from Argentina, Georgia and

Italy, blended with young, home-grown talent, has given the Dens Park faithful some optimism that there are even better days ahead, and has resulted undoubtedly in the best football to be played at Dens in many years.

They are now in a position where they are attracting international players, but in order to balance the wage bill, it has already been necessary for Dundee to sell whenever a decent offer for a player comes along; Caniggia was sold to Rangers within a year.

On their day, Dundee are capable of winning against any team in the Scottish Premier League, but they are equally capable of losing. Despite this inconsistency, for the first time in a generation, Dundee fans can claim to be the city's stronger club without worrying about the provisions of the Mental Health Act.

A FEW STATISTICS

Ground: Dens Park
Capacity: 11,200
Current ticket price: Adult £16
Address: Sandeman Street, Dundee
Tel. No.: 01382 889966
Ticketline: 01382 889774
Website: www.dundeefc.co.uk

Manager: Ivano Bonetti (since season 2000–2001)
Strip: Home – dark-blue top, white shorts, dark-blue socks
  Away – White top with blue vertical stripes, dark–blue shorts and dark–blue socks
Top scorer: Alan Gilzean – 163 goals in 181 games
Biggest win: 10–0 versus Alloa 1946–7; 10–0 versus Dunfermline 1946–47
Biggest defeat: 0–11 versus Celtic 1895–96

Selected Trophies/Achievements
Scottish League champions 1961–62
Scottish FA Cup winners 1909–10
Scottish League Cup winners 1951–52, 1952–53,
European Champions Cup semi-finalists 1962–63
Scottish League Centenary Cup winners 1990–91

Further Reading
Bonetti's Blues – Jim Wilkie (Mainstream)
Across the Great Divide – Jim Wilkie (Mainstream)
Dundee Greats – Jim Hendry (Sportsprint)
Up Wi' the Bonnets! (The Centenary History of Dundee FC) – Norrie
Price

Football and Pies by Crusty Dog

Despite early doubts, I am a true lover of the Scotch pie. The word
'Scotch' is only acceptable in two situations – one is when talking
about drams, the other in reference to the pie. As a regular travelling
football fan, I often partake in a pie at the game. Needless to say, some
are more enjoyable than others. There are some fine steak pies at Killie
and Motherwell (steak pies are at the top end of the market). Whilst
Dundee United do a fair mutton pie and a fine bridie, they're usually
sold out too early. This is a common problem: 'nae hot food' when you
really fancy some. Dunfermline Athletic serve up a rare steak bridie,
St Johnstone do a good pie, and I remember a rather miserable trip to
Old Boghead, Dumbarton, being illuminated by a mutton pie.
Football pies worth swerving are Ayr United's virtually raw mutton
affairs. Hearts' were, in my experience, always over-cooked and dried
out. Any Old Firm product, given that it comes in corporate
packaging, is second rate, and should be avoided.

Gay Dundee

Not a lot of choice and, strangely, all are very handy for the bus station.

LIBERTY'S NIGHTCLUB
124 Seagate
Tel: 01382 200660
(See 'Clubs' section)

BAR XS
124 Seagate
Tel: 01382 200660

As you may have guessed from the address, Bar XS is attached to Liberty's. It's open seven nights a week – with a quiz night on Monday, bingo on Tuesday and a karaoke night on Friday. It also acts as a pre-club bar for Liberty's and grants you £1 off entry to it if entering from here.

CHARLIE'S BAR
75 Seagate
Tel: 01382 226840

Formerly The Gauger, this remains a traditional and popular, if unremarkable pub. Fairly spacious, with some pool tables. It's also handy for Marks and Spencer.

Haircuts

How can you recommend a hairdresser without running the risk of them becoming so popular that you never get an appointment there again? There are around 100 places to get a haircut in Dundee (if you've read the section on Albert Street shops, you'll understand how this is). It's a very personal thing I feel, and having been with the same hairdresser for around ten years I'm slightly biased. Here are a few.

BARBERS
13 Union Street
Tel: 01382 229250

My personal choice, but I'm not telling you who actually cuts my hair. Big mirrors and chairs, good sounds and coffee, and they use a very inventive elasticated paper collar to stop the hair tickling your back for the next three days. Thankfully, conversation very rarely touches on the subject of holidays. Barbers comes recommended by many besides myself. They have recently opened a baby Barbers at the bottom of the street, on Whitehall Crescent. It's not for babies, it's just smaller.

There are also good reports about the following:

MERCHANTS
46 Murraygate
Tel: 01382 228870

McINTYRES
121 Perth Road
Tel: 01382 668077
and also at
50 Union Street
Tel: 01382 202080

HQ'S HAIRDRESSING
37 Cowgate
Tel. 01382 227474

CHARLIE TAYLOR
95–101 Nethergate
Tel: 01382 909090

Ice Cream

Dundee – or rather Broughty Ferry – is rightly famous for Visocchi's ice cream. Since opening in 1954, they have been providing the public with their unsurpassable vanilla variety. It is sublime, but impossible to do justice to in the written word, so just get yourself down there and sample it for yourself. You can now get just about any flavour imaginable, but my heart will always belong to vanilla. My first choice of presentation was always a 'slider' – two wafers with a big slab of ice cream between their wafery walls. Cones, also known as 'pokey hats', are probably safer, but not as much fun. Visocchi's (affectionately known as 'V's when I was younger), now also has a mouth-watering range of Italian cakes and chocolate, as well as an extensive menu of pizza and pasta dishes (see 'Cafés' section).

Michael Marra

Agreed, individual people don't really count as 'what to do and where to do it', but you can't write a book about Dundee without including the finest singer-songwriter in Scotland (who just happens to be from Dundee, by the way). Witty, thoughtful, poetic, and sometimes just plain daft, his songs are often, but not exclusively, written in Dundee vernacular. The remarkable talent he has for lyric writing had led to recognition not just Scotland-wide, but world-wide. Not one to be pigeon-holed (people have tried and failed), he has been described as 'the Randy Newman of the north', and likened to Tom Waits (gruff voices and good stories). If pushed to find a description for him, it would probably be 'entertainer'. There's always a story behind his songs and although the albums exist beautifully in their own right, I would encourage anyone with an interest in good storytelling and songsmithing to go and see him live. The next time you listen to the records, the experience will be all the richer. He used to play in his baffies (slippers), but apparently you can't find a zipped baffy these days for love nor money. He does, however, continue to play live with his keyboard on an ironing board.

As this book is about Dundee, I'll only mention Dundee-specific songs. 'General Grant's Visit to Dundee' is based on a real happening, but imbued with fairytale status; 'Frida Kahlo's Visit to the Taybridge Bar' has been mentioned previously in the Taybridge Bar review (a beautiful song, made all the more sweet if you know the pub, Frida Kahlo, and particularly Jimmy Howie). One of Marra's football songs has been mentioned in the 'Football' section: 'Hamish the Goalie', written as a commemorative 'hymn' on the occasion of the Dundee United goalie's testimonial, which famously was attended by Grace Kelly. (Grace Kelly! She didn't go to Ibrox, you know.) Slightly more bizarre is that Leo Sayer did a cover of 'Hamish'. For singalong numbers, you can't beat the legendary 'Hermless', which Michael himself introduces as a contender for the new national anthem. What a day that would be.

He also co-wrote and produced the definitive 'Dundee' album, Saint Andrew's *The Word on the Pavey*, which has a full lyric booklet with a Dundee glossary. Songs include 'Ananinginaneana' and 'It's Rare T'Be Alehv (is it)'.

Music

Other notable bands and singers to have come out of Dundee over the years are:

Danny Wilson – three Dundee boys who had their biggest moment with 'Mary's Prayer' in 1988.

Billy MacKenzie – the late Dundee maverick who found fame with his band The Associates.

Tayside Police Pipe Band – success worldwide.

Average White Band – most famous for 'Pick up the Pieces'.

Deacon Blue – Hits include 'Dignity' and 'Raintown'. Singer Ricky Ross also wrote a song for Dundee United called 'Proud to be an Arab'.

Pies

Growing up in Dundee, a pie was traditional Saturday lunch. Often eaten cold, they were an absolute delight as a child; naturally we had no reason to question their content. It had to be, of course, a Wallace's Pie – nothing else would do. Sometimes a sausage roll was brought in as a substitute (and even the occasional bridie) – but a Dundee *peh* was the thing that really hit the spot. Whether eaten cold from its paper bag, or heated up and presented like a castle within a moat of beans, this was our 'living for the weekend'. A friend and I regularly went ice skating on a Saturday morning, and were sent off by my gran with two paper bags each, one containing a *peh*, the other a meringue. Cue Dundee joke:

'Is that a pie or a meringue?'

'No, you were right the first time.'

Post Offices

The traditional post office seems to be becoming a dying breed. The first big one I noticed going was the Broughty Ferry post office which I really liked. This is now a pub, and not a very good one in my opinion. I preferred it when it smelled of stamps and Family Allowance books. The post office in the Ferry now operates from the former R.S. McColl's newsagent in Brook Street. The impressive building on Ward Road which used to house the city's main post office has recently been turned into a nightclub called The Circus, and the *Tully* sellers you used to see on the steps have been replaced by burly bouncers. The post office has just been shoved a bit to the right of its former home, with none of the authority of the original. Other wee post offices around town have adopted secondary occupations. The one on Victoria Road used to operate as a Butlin's booking centre, then it branched out into small girls' leotards, and hand-knitted baby clothes. At the time of writing it is up for sale. Albert Street post office was mentioned previously in the street's entry in the 'Where to Shop' section. Toys, games, loads of cards, and stationery await you in this branch.

Potted Hough

There's a delicacy called potted hough (sometimes known as butcher's hough) and the only two beings I knew who ate this were my brother and our dog. It's a greyish-brown lump of jellified leftovers, sold in ribbed plastic tubs, and it looks absolutely foul. I know it's not exclusive to Dundee, but it will always remind me of growing up here. It can be bought at most butchers and also in McLeish's.

Public Toilets

As the possessor of a fairly small bladder, knowing where I can stop off for a pee is quite high on my list of priorities when visiting any town. It's not so much spending a 'penny' nowadays, though, as 20p. However, peeing in public can still be a free experience if you know where to go.

Overgate Centre Thumbs-up all round here. These loos are free, always spotlessly clean and for once there are an ample number of cubicles in the ladies – I'm sure all the 'ladies' out there will agree that this is an unusual but very welcome feature. The cubicles are also fantastically roomy; none of this struggling to squeeze yourself between the door/pan/sanitary bin, with or without your bags of shopping. You are also given a choice of paper towel or hand dryer (this is important for the hand-dryer haters out there). There is a full-length mirror for you to check out how you're bearing up after a long, hard shop.

Wellgate Centre. These used to cost 20p, but have recently become free. Obviously too much competition. There are twelve cubicles, but remarkably only two hand dryers and no alternative. So you may not have to queue to pee, but there will be a fight at the sinks. No frills, but clean.

Customer Toilets

BHS This store kindly provides free toilets for their customers. If you're up this end of town, and find yourself not just caught short but short of 20p, you can pose briefly as a customer before slipping discreetly into their loos. They're not particularly exciting, but they do the job so to speak. And they're free.

Arnotts Again, free toilets for customers. They've been recently refurbished, although it would take a well-trained eye to notice what exactly has been upgraded. All the fittings look as though they've been repaired and re-repaired many times. Badly. There's also always a faint whiff lingering here. However, when you're desperate, you don't always care, and it's somewhere to park yourself.

Debenhams We can see a pattern emerging here in the customer toilets department. Yes, these too are free, and are very pleasant. They have the advantage of being new, as with the Overgate's own loos, but they seem well maintained, clean, and with that hand-towel versus hand-dryer contest looming ever larger, they sit on the fence and generously offer both.

On the Street

Don't take this too literally, please. This covers traditional public toilets which you can stumble across whilst walking, and not just shopping.

Castle Street Provided by the council, these are good traditional fare, with lots of tiles and cubicles. The cost was 20p the last time I went in.

Westport They're something of a landmark, these pyramid toilets. I've never ventured in, as the thought of descending into their underground depths doesn't really appeal to me. I'm told they're fairly standard, unremarkable toilets. But if you're in the area, and feel the need, I'm sure they'll be a welcome sight.

Broughty Ferry Car Park Across the road from Broughty Ferry library (the design of which was based on the Petit Trianon at the Palais de Versailles) are some award-winning toilets. They're in a car park, but don't let that put you off. These are very clean, well-cared-for loos, with an attempt at making it a pleasant experience for the user. They have artificial plants here to brighten the place up.

Seagulls

Being on the coast, Dundee has more than its fair share of seagulls. They are not an uncommon sight for such a location, but *these* seagulls are very, very big. They're also fearless beasts; you certainly wouldn't pick a fight with one of them – I've seen them fighting each other outside the local nature reserve (aka McDonald's) – and all for the remains of a flaccid bap. Indeed, if you ever find yourself walking through the city centre early in the morning, before Dundee's extremely efficient cleansing department has started work, you will see much evidence of what has produced these oversized beasts: kebabs, fish suppers, and a surprising amount of white cabbage, as well as the aforementioned burger buns. Drunk and hungry, the late-night drinker, unable to coordinate hand and mouth, will usually have dropped around 75 per cent of his

midnight feast. Gull heaven, I imagine. And just the other day, I saw a seagull in the centre of town tucking into an entire packet of chocolate digestives – true. Whatever the reason, these gulls are enormous and not to be messed with. Imagine the terror a friend of mine felt when she woke up one day to find one in the middle of her living-room (19 floors up in a multi), sitting on her phone book . . . Legend has it, also, that a seagull in the Hilltown once swallowed a cocker spaniel in one mouthful.

Prepare to be dive-bombed, physically and splatteringly, by these beautiful but cocky birds.

Seals

Seals have been spotted up and down the River Tay. If you're in Dundee and look towards the rail bridge rather than the road one, you might just be lucky enough to see the odd seal family basking on the sand banks when the tide's low. It's not exactly an everyday occurrence though, so if seals are your thing, you may want to go further afield. I had a word with our local Seal Pup, who gave some advice on the subject.

The best thing to do if you want to check out the local seal population is to head over to Tentsmuir. Cross the Tay Bridge and simply head for Tayport and the Tentsmuir woods. There's a signposted path to direct you through the woods; turn left to trace the curve of the shoreline. The sea will soon be visible, and you can cut through the woods, and head for the beach at any point. The sands are increasingly beautiful as you move further away from Tayport, and stretch for miles. This area is a protected nature reserve and a blissful escapist treat from the city. When the tide is out, you should be able to see the schools of seals that lie by the water's edge, dozens of big, brown soppy-eyed lumps that sing their high-pitched eerie songs. If you approach them quietly and slowly, they'll stare at you for a while before flobbering away into the water. I once got off the train at Leuchars to walk back to Dundee along the sands. By the time I reached the beach, a thick mist had descended, and through the swirly clouds, I could hear their spooky cries, which was a little unnerving to say the least. Occasionally a school of dolphins appears in the Tay, which spurs the local press into all sorts of bad puns about a new school opening in Dundee, and how the pupils are having a whale of a time. Maybe just as well they don't turn up more often.

Skating

DUNDEE ICE ARENA
Camperdown Leisure Complex
Kingsway West
Tel: 01382 608060

Poor old Dundee was without an ice rink for a number of years, following the closure of the old ice rink, which, if you've read the section on 'Pies', you'll know I used to frequent as a lass. The new rink (sorry, arena) is bigger and swankier, with all sorts of additional facilities such as a function suite, sports bar and snack bar. There's also a shop and skate-sharpening service should you find you're not cutting any ice, so to speak. They now have, apparently, an olympic size ice 'pad', where you can come to watch ice-hockey matches or local skating champs of tomorrow spinning their shiny trousers. If you just fancy a good old skate round, opening hours for public skating vary, and is not always on full ice. The skate discos on Friday and Saturday nights sound good. As ever, check for details.

Swimming

OLYMPIA LEISURE CENTRE
Earl Grey Place
Tel: 01382 434888

The Olympia Leisure Centre is in some ways very good and in others very poor. In *Kingdom by the Sea*, Paul Theroux's classic account of his travels around Britain, his passage on Dundee is limited to an exceedingly unflattering description of the Olympia building and its Stalinesque attributes. I used to swim here quite often, and have quite a fondness for the place. The temperature of the water is unpredictable, the chlorine levels seem to waver somewhat, but it has a good-sized training pool, usually not too busy, with some great characters. A good time to swim is between 8.30 a.m. onwards; by this time the pre-work swimmers have departed, and the second shift has not yet arrived. This kicks off around 9 a.m. with an influx of more mature swimmers, usually on great form, always up for a chat, and prone to singing *very* loudly in the showers. There is a large leisure pool with waves, flumes, rapid rivers, inflatable things, and all the fun family stuff. A separate shallow pool is provided for parents to gently introduce their small children to the joys of learning to swim. There is also a gym at the Olympia which is good value, although you will be subjected to music that you probably won't want to hear (lots of John Lennon, which doesn't really inspire rapid movement). There's a sauna and solarium too.

A PERSONAL SWIMMING ACCOUNT by Doggy Paddle

One of my most memorable times at Olympia was witnessing the lifesaving classes that ran for several weeks over the summer. The class consisted of around ten youths – mostly an assortment of gangly, seemingly malnourished young men, a couple of overweight boys, and one girl – all appalling swimmers. The boys were at the 'I don't like my body and I am profoundly embarrassed because that girl's wearing a bikini' stage. Lots of mumbling and eye contact avoidance ensued, neither helpful in the art of life saving. After much standing around and shivering, the class members were paired up and instructed to enact drowning scenarios. What followed was both hilarious, and, should you ever be in the unfortunate position of drowning, very worrying. My favourite scenario involved the girl, who, resplendent in her bikini, obviously had a fair amount of bare flesh on show. She played the drowning role, shrieking in Penelope Pitstop fashion. Her partner flung himself into the water, moving towards her by means of a swimming stroke I was not yet acquainted with and more suited to Labradors. General panic and flailing ensued, with the boy in an evident state of panic over the prospect of bodily contact. He refused to hold her, and she swallowed lots of water. Should the scenario have been carried to its logical conclusion, death most certainly would have resulted. However, the instructor happily intervened, and all was well. The classes continued into the summer, each with similar scenarios of entertaining ineptitude and a phenomenal amount of unnecessary splashing. I considered writing a television series based on the Olympia lifesaving classes. It would have been called 'Taywatch', but I suspect the audience would have been limited.

Other places you can swim in Dundee:

LOCHEE LEISURE AND SWIMMING CENTRE
St Mary's Lane
Lochee
Tel: 01382 432690

DUNDEE UNIVERSITY
Tel: 01382 344122/3
Limited times for public swimming. Check for details.

Useful Information

TOURIST INFORMATION
21 Castle Street
Tel: 01382 527527

Taxis

As with any city, Dundee has an abundance of taxi firms. Most can be picked up on the street and at designated taxi ranks dotted around town. Main ones are outside the City Churches, McManus Galleries and the railway station. There is also a new firm with a fleet of silver Mercedes, which is a pleasant way to get around. At time of writing, you can't pick these up on the street, but only by booking first.

Some taxi firms I've used, and would use again are:

Tele Taxis
Tel: 01382 669333/889333
Handy Taxis
Tel: (free no) 0500 303060
Dundee Taxi Cabs (silver Merc boys)
Tel: 01382 203020
Mitchells Taxis
Tel: 01382 623623
Tay Taxis
Tel: 01382 458000/450450

Broughty Ferry Taxis
Tel: 01382 477255
Discovery Taxis
Tel: 01382 732111

Buses

For local buses, contact Travel Dundee. They're genuinely helpful, and can give you information on any bus within Dundee city, and some Broughty Ferry buses.

Strathtay operate most of the buses that go outwith the city, including the Monifieth, Carnoustie and Arbroath buses, which are also good ones to use to get to Broughty Ferry, and they are more direct than the Dundee ones. There are also buses to Newport and Tayport, Forfar, Glamis and a host of other destinations. For information, either pop into the Seagate Bus Station for timetables, or phone Strathtay direct.

TRAVEL DUNDEE
Tel: 01382 201121/450002

STRATHTAY
Tel: 01382 228345

You can get information on the following services at Seagate Bus Station, or phone directly.

STAGECOACH
Tel: 01738 629339

CITYLINK
Tel: 08705 505050

NATIONAL EXPRESS
Tel: 08705 808080

Trains

You can no longer phone Dundee station directly. For telephone enquiries, you have to go through National Rail Enquiries. You can catch a train directly to Aberdeen, Glasgow, Perth and Edinburgh, and some go directly to London, Birmingham and Bristol, although many of the longer-distance journeys will require a change at Edinburgh. Staff at Dundee railway station are pretty friendly and helpful on the whole, and will do their best to get you the cheapest fare possible, despite the ridiculous restrictions on most of these tickets.

NATIONAL RAIL ENQUIRIES
0845 7484950

Dundee Airport

Possibly the best airport in Britain, with daily flights between Dundee and London City airport, the most central of them all. If you're in the West End, particularly near Magdalen Green, and ask for directions to the airport, they may go something like this: 'Go to the bottom of your street, cross the bridge, turn right, and it's a ten-minute walk from there.' A friend duly followed these instructions, and walked straight past it. It is absolutely tiny. There are no shops, tourists, terrible food halls, theme bars, or any miscellaneous airport horrors. What they do have are newspapers, coffee, tea and biscuits – all of which are free – and somewhere comfy to sit. The staff are great, and once you've checked in, the cheery security man will invite you to help yourself to the aforementioned refreshments. The flight between Dundee and London is stunning, and takes about an hour. At one point, you can look down and see both the River Tay and the Firth of Forth. On your return to Dundee, you can easily walk to the city centre in half an hour or so, should you feel the need to stretch your legs.

DUNDEE AIRPORT
Tel: 01382 643242

SCOT AIRWAYS
Tel: 0870 6060707

Local Media

NEWSPAPERS

Dundee Courier: Contains local news, including many photos of children and fundraising events. Catch up on who's been jailed for what, and for how long. Covers the basics of national and world news. Certain days are good for advertisements – whether you want to rent a flat, or buy a guinea pig. Friday is jobs day. Also includes 'What's On' listings. A fairly inoffensive newspaper, and good for local sport.

Evening Telegraph: Known as 'the *Tully*', this is a tabloid-sized, and very thin version of the *Courier*, with even less news. Favourite features are the letters page, and the teatime mini quiz. Occasionally has great headlines, such as 'Brain Abandoned in Dundee Car Park'. True.

Sunday Post: Harmless, family fare with minimal amount of news. Its enduring appeal is down to *Oor Wullie* and *The Broons*.

Local publishing tycoons are responsible for the production of tons of comics and magazines, most famously *The Beano* and *The Dandy*. Other perennial favourites are the *People's Friend* and girls' comics such as *Bunty*, and teenage magazines. My earliest claim to fame is to have featured in one of the early photo stories in *My Guy*. It was a special Valentine's Day issue, and I played a lovesick Victorian girl.

Well, we all have to start somewhere. I think most folk in Dundee appeared in one of these at one time or another.

RADIO

Dundee has two local commercial radio stations. Both play music.

Radio Tay: Well-established and useful for local information on weather and traffic reports.

Wave 102: Dundee's new radio station, again with a local focus.

TELEVISION

Channel 6: Dundee's own wee TV station, this is a fairly recent enterprise. Currently it shows mostly music videos, cartoons and some very poor (but highly entertaining) local ads.

Bibliography

The Rough Guide to Scotland, 5th edition
Footprint Guide to Scotland, 2nd edition
Smiling School for Calvinists by Bill Duncan, Bloomsbury plc
Dundee Pubs Past and Present by John Alexander
Dundee: A Voyage of Discovery, edited by Graham Ogilvy, Mainstream

(Permission to use Michael Marra lyrics given by Peggy Marra)

All illustrations by Chris Biddlecombe
All photographs by Malcolm J. Thomson, Studio M, Dundee

Index